THE TYPE 3 COMPANY

The Type 3 Company

Georges Archier
and Hervé Sérieyx

Translated by
Michael Johnson

NICHOLS PUBLISHING COMPANY : NEW YORK

HD
58.9
.A7313
1987

© Gower Publishing Company Limited 1987

First published in the United States of America in 1987 by
Nichols Publishing Company,
Post Office Box 96,
New York, N.Y. 10024

Library of Congress Cataloging-in-Publication Data

Archier, Georges
  The type 3 company.
  Translation of: L'entreprise du 3e type.
  1. Organizational effectiveness – Case studies.
  2. Organizational change – Case studies.
I. Sérieyx, Hervé.   II. Title.
  HD58.9.A7313   1987   658'.00973   87–11203

ISBN 0–89397–282–7

Printed in Great Britain.

Contents

Illustrations

Figures

Tables

Foreword

by K W Humphreys, Chairman and Managing Director, May & Baker Ltd

As head of the British subsidiary of a major French company I was particularly interested to read the proofs of Georges Archier and Hervé Sérieyx' new book. A number of Anglo-Saxon authors have looked at excellent companies to analyse their reasons for success and though the French authors have used a different philosophical process, their conclusions are clearly compatible.

The result of their analysis is a clear and concise summary of the management techniques used by successful modern companies and provides a valuable checklist for those wishing to improve performance, a sort of Michelin Guide to modern management practices.

Japanese companies have been accepted as the best performers for some years and it has almost become folk-lore to believe Western companies cannot, for cultural reasons, follow the same methods. I was delighted therefore to find US and French Companies quoted alongside Japanese examples.

It is good to read of such cases. Many companies, including my own, have been striving to open up management processes, to generate greater employee involvement through consultative systems, briefing, quality circles and so on. We have had successes and set-backs, recognizing that attitudes on all sides need to change. The difficulties of introducing democracy should not be under-estimated and the time-scale for success can be long. Often managers find it hard to consult rather than instruct; status is felt to be lost.

This book makes a great contribution to these developments as it pulls together the various strands into a logical whole, setting clear guidelines for implementation. It argues logically that change is vital – after all, society has changed and business, an important, integral part of our society, must change with it. People have more knowledge and freedom than ever before and wish to use it in their working life, to be treated as intelligent, contributing members of an organization.

The Type 3 Company was originally published in French in 1985 and has been a great success. I have no doubt that this excellent English translation will be equally successful. It has the great virtue, compared to most books on management, of being short, easy to read and yet full of important messages. I commend it to all who aspire to manage a successful, modern company.

Preface

It is often said that our competitors in the Far East will soon run into trouble as a result of their explosive growth in recent years – and that our industries in Europe will enjoy a new period of resurgence. It is also said that our governments will reduce burdensome taxes and social costs and give us more scope to expand our businesses.

This kind of thinking is rooted in the belief that our companies are blessed with a system that is basically sound, and moving in the right direction, as proved by a history of high performance. The only problem seems to be that there are several outside sources of pressure acting on us simultaneously. There is a crisis, but it will pass.

Here is an alternative view of the situation. This is not a crisis, it is much more serious: in fact we are living through a period of radical change in society and industrial activity on a global scale. The main changes are technological (computerization, and information as a major new resource), sociological (better educated young people) and competitive (the new powerhouses of Asia).

What some regard as temporary constraints imposed from outside are actually the new facts of life. This great transformation, dramatized in the 1970s by the oil-price increases, will require at least another ten years to settle down. The changes are both internal and external, and they are in a state of rapid flux. The truth is that the conditions of the past will never return, except in very limited ways. As a result, companies must adapt their concepts and their methods to achieve short-term success and to prepare for future challenges.

Of course the present is the first priority. Winning today's battles is of paramount importance, but this can only be done by setting aside the old mentality, together with traditional ideas about structure, relations between various parts of the organization, management methods, and maybe other things.

A company seeking better performance through change must answer two key questions: what to change, and how to change it. As for what to change, two options are open: to experiment with original solutions or to survey the industrialized world for solutions that already work and borrow them. There is much to learn from successful companies – those that are producing economic and social progress, those that have overcome problems more traditional companies have failed to master. This has been the direction of our research over the past several years, and it has led us to study a large number of dynamic companies in Europe, the United States, Japan and South Korea.

This book presents the essence of our observations. It is not a book of reflections from an ivory tower but a report on field observations. We offer 'strategies for progress' common to companies operating in different countries and different cultures; and we also suggest some methods, all of them based on reality, not on untested theory. We have not attempted an exhaustive study. Our emphasis is on the management of people, products, progress, and the relation with the outside environment. We do not discuss financial management – not because we underestimate its importance but because we believe that other areas have greater potential for generating the kind of change we feel companies need today.

Lastly, this book concentrates on the manager's own scope for increasing growth and performance, not what other forces, or other institutions, might or should do.

Our book examines five main themes:

1   The *battles that must be won* for a company to survive.

2   *Groupings inside companies* – managers must realize that

they can no longer win their battles alone or even with the help of their general staff, however competent it may be. They must harness the support, the ideas and the energy of the frontline troops so that responsibility for all their projects is shared. It becomes an experiment in communal living, a new way to use time, requiring the mobilization of all the creative resources of the company, for the faster and more complete satisfaction of the customer.

3   *Company groupings*. In a similar way companies will need to pool ideas and resources. This can be achieved by establishing 'networks of leaders', as we illustrate through three remarkable case studies.

4   *Group management*. It is not enough to bring ideas together. The best of them must be selected, and ways must be found to share them both throughout the group of companies and within each of them. This is the mission that falls to a new type of management – the management of progress inside the company and within a group of companies – and is a new attribute of the high-performance company, which we call a Type 3 company.

5   *How to begin*. We shall show that a company can start from any of several points. With patience, determination, perseverance, pragmatism and a modicum of humility towards the ideas of others, and a willingness to trust them, one can begin with any of the strands, provided it leads to progress of a kind needed by the company. By pulling this first string, the entire ball of necessary changes can eventually be unravelled.

Finally, we must caution against harbouring illusions about the capacities of our traditional industrial system. Type 3 companies already exist. Some are taking shape in Europe, and many exist in other parts of the world. They have copied the classic Taylor-based system of organization but they have improved on it, retaining the good points and discarding the errors. In Asia they have duplicated our main industrial products and they sell them worldwide at a better quality/ price ratio. Tomorrow they will do the same in new areas. Above all, they will have perfected the new products they are at this moment developing – unless, that is, we prove ourselves capable of designing them ourselves, and then producing and distributing them with a new kind of company that is both more efficient and more humane.

Georges Archier
Hervé Sérieyx

Introduction: new challenges, new responses

Actually the new challenges are not that new. From 1945 to 1975 Europe experienced thirty years of industrial reconstruction and growth, during which companies, preoccupied with their need for materials, allowed contradictions to take deeper and deeper root in their structures and their activities. As a result they were in no position to respond to the challenges this produced. From 1976, with reconstruction behind them but suffering the effects of oil shocks on energy costs, European companies faced a flood of goods from Asia, which finally highlighted these contradictions and presented new challenges that seemed almost impossible to meet.

From this period, we note seven main contradictions:

1 Salary expectations v job satisfaction

Two or three generations ago, when the educational system was less developed, many workers expected from their employers only basic compensation. Today's workers are much better educated in general knowledge and in technology. They face a constant flow of information on every conceivable subject from the media, and enjoy a wide choice of consumer goods. Consequently our generation has neither the same needs nor expectations as earlier ones in private or working life. All sociological studies confirm that growing members of workers want to evolve with a living organization, and to perform useful work, in a 'transparent' organization. They want a congenial work atmosphere, and above all they want to use their knowledge and their imagination to improve both their standard of living and the results of their work, mainly by taking more initiative. They are more and more hostile to ideologies and ready-made systems. They want to play a part in the making of their environment and their lives.

At first companies felt they had no reason to try to satisfy the new needs of their employees. Workers were originally unskilled people with minimal qualification who could become productive with a minimum of training. Work was broken down into a chain of small tasks, and machinery was developed to implement these concepts and to make the operating procedures as devoid as possible of responsibility. The system was developed to extremes, so that specialities became increasingly narrow and career development was restrained; these structural barriers were rigid – vertically between functions and horizontally between categories.

This approach worked well for over a century, making mass production possible for the first time in the history of mankind and allowing the West to siphon off riches from the underdeveloped world. Thus it is not so difficult to understand companies' attachment to the old system, by which they hope to continue to produce profit. Even their resistance to change is natural, although the impact of change on their workers is irreversible.

These contradictions are at the root of the conflicts that exist within industry:

- The profound boredom with meaningless and monotonous work; the rejection of special categories such as workers, employees, foremen, supervisors; and the disparity in the status and privileges accorded to each.

- The desire for a guaranteed salary: where there is no possibility of sharing in the life of the company by means of a system that creates involvement, this is the worker's only source of compensation.

In summary, a company today must secure the commitment

of its personnel to improve its performance. Today's workers are more and more prepared to contribute their intelligence and their ideas. But despite this, conflict worsens because the industrial system is in large part inadequate and out of date.

2   Social considerations v 'the bottom line'

It's surprising how many business people still think the financial performance of a company is separate and distinct from its role in society. They think of the social role as subordinate to the economic, which often leads to a concentration of effort on 'bottom line' performance. They do not realize that our precarious social balance depends on social progress. Social aims are seen as an expense, economic aims as income. But in fact the social side is critical: its importance lies in the quality of work life and the possibility of those who work to contribute and apply their own perception of progress. For a long time the employee has been considered the muscles of the company. He is still thought of like that, but more and more he is coming to be seen as a brain as well.

3   Innovation v imitation

How did the Western world allow itself to be outperformed by countries that only twenty years ago were considered underdeveloped? We in Europe were careful to perfect our system and refine it after trips to the United States. We were convinced of the system's superiority, but we allowed ourselves to be overtaken, saying 'They pay such low salaries' or 'They only copy us', and 'We shall pull ahead again when they have finished copying everything'. But the contradiction is still there: their salaries are approaching ours, they are developing new products, and their productivity continues to grow faster than ours.

4   Productivity v employment

Our companies are torn between two seemingly contradictory imperatives: on the one hand the vital need to improve productivity and thereby reduce employment, and on the other society's requirement to achieve full employment. This conflict today sparks endless debates inside companies and poisons relations between employers and governments. Official solutions have proved ineffective. A more reasonable approach might be to make the maximum possible productivity improvement, then to share the gain in several ways: salary increases, investment in the company, lower selling price, and more employment. But of course we cannot ignore the competitive pressures from other companies that are improving their quality/cost ratio and rapidly increasing their share of market.

5 Flexibility v rigidity

Flexibility is one of the hallmarks of a successful company. Everyone agrees that companies must be flexible, agile and responsive to keep up with the changing marketplace and the constantly shifting needs of customers. This flexibility is as important in company structure as in the mobility of the personnel, and it is essential to the research and development team, which must be alert for changing tastes and new production techniques to satisfy them rapidly. Yet companies today are hampered by a variety of shackles. Some are internal: e.g. the pyramid structure of departments and services that are less and less integrated, vertical and horizontal barriers, outdated professional classification, handbooks of inefficient operational procedures, and floods of memos. Some are external: e.g. government regulations that tend to make all activities conform to a uniform standard.

On the one hand, we all say we favour mobility, initiative, entrepreneurial managers. But on the other hand, we also, out of a sense of caution, accept regulation and detailed control of all activities. Companies competing in the world marketplace today are like athletes – some carrying heavy weights, some not – and in the running and jumping events the difference in performance will be considerable.

6 Image v real role

No one questions the essential role of industry in the creation of wealth – products and services, workers' earnings, investment capital, and taxes for the benefit of the community. It is industry that contributes, along with other institutions, so much to the economic and social image of a nation. Industry produces more than products. It produces people, citizens, skills, professional and social growth. Yet the image of industry is poor, and industry is under attack even from within. In addition to internal conflicts industry suffers from its image as a generator of profits. We say we want a dynamic industrial community that makes massive contributions to the state, yet the paradox is that profitability has a bad image, and it is getting worse.

7 Management education v business reality

The education system trains professionals as specialists, but more and more companies want the generalist. We develop individualists but companies want managers who work well in groups. We are adding new courses to business education programmes but business complains that education is lagging behind current requirements – especially in the humanities.

The new approach

Most companies are still wrestling with some or all of the contradictions listed above. Throughout the postwar period managers have been experimenting with new ideas, trying to keep pace with change.

As we indicated earlier, the norm for industrial companies in all industrialized countries was the separation of work tasks – the separation of managers, who organize, from the subordinates, who execute – the Taylor system. The organization comes first, then the employees; power is held by specialized management teams and by the leader who dominates the pyramid; the workers are one resource among many; and quality is checked by a *post facto* quality-control system. By now, we know the system does not work.

Many companies have tried to implement solutions that might be called 'Taylorism tamed', in which the industrial machinery has been 'oiled' according to need but the basic

Taylorite concepts retained. In fighting the erosion of productivity and disaffection with work life some methods have
been imported from the United States – streamlining of tasks
and other productivity measures. To reduce conflict with
labour unions and to work towards the elusive consensus
improvements in human relations were introduced. To the
same end we had management by objectives (MBO). In response to the great waves of social change of our era, we
have recently witnessed efforts to improve working conditions
and the encouragement of dialogue with workers, but it is
clear that industry has not changed fundamentally. The aim
is still financial gain, and the role of the manager and worker
remain separate. Taylorism remains intact. The real
challenges of our time are not being faced.

Another set of solutions, quite different form the first,
might be called Taylor II. These are applied by state-owned
companies, who fulfil their destiny in carrying out centralized
planning directives. They live in a world of socio-economic
ideology that decides their production objectives, defines their
role and determines their compensation. Taylor II is even
more handicapped by its spurious logic than the original.
Taylor II companies don't face the same contradictions as
ordinary companies, because the state protects them from
the world of free competition and to some degree the world
of free expression. The results have been questionable, in
terms of both economic performance and job satisfaction.
Certainly the Taylor II companies do not have a reputation
for high performance in either field, and the other Taylorite
companies retain their roots in the old, outdated system.

The only way out is to seek solutions that are not based
on Taylorism, and rather than attempt to invent a new system
from scratch, we have gone to the companies that have dealt
successfully with modern contradictions and conflicts.
Actually there are many good examples in Europe, the United
States and of course in Japan and elsewhere that have found
new approaches in nearly all areas of work to improve performance and competitiveness – in short, to enter the third
avenue of evolution. We call these the Type 3 companies.
They expand their market share because their products benefit
from the best combination of service, quality and price. They

know how to identify, fight and win internal battles for the loyalty and commitment of their employees and external battles of competition and technological progress. To summarize, these battles are:

- The humanization of the enterprise so as to offer today's employees the quality of life they deserve.

- Simultaneous and synergistic social and economic progress, the one feeding the other.

- Progress in technology and in innovation to maintain full employment.

- A renewal of leadership in industrial management.

- The rehabilitation of the manufacturing company as the essential core of the developed countries.

- Massive re-education of managers, by means of in-company training programmes.

Type 3 companies have all paid their respects to Taylorism for the virtue it once offered, but now have turned towards the future, saying 'Goodbye, Mr Taylor'.

Until recently the industrial battle was fought exclusively by the 'generals' – top management, financiers, technicians – but things have changed. The message from all the leading industrialized countries is the same, and their industrial companies are beginning to make it real: the winners will be those who learn to mobilize their one key resource, manpower.

It is happening in Japan and California, at Komatsu, Nippon Steel, Nissan, at Tandem, Apple Computer, Hewlett-Packard, at Mitsubishi, IBM and MITI, at the venture capital companies. It is becoming clear that the intelligence, the critical faculties, the commitment, the dreams, the creativity, all the richness and diversity available to us, must be mobilized. It is the only way to be competitive today.

In other words, the Taylorite approach to management has had its day, and it is time to throw it on the scrap heap. Along with it we must jettison the concept of 'managers who think' and 'workers who follow orders'.

For Europe this could be a case of lucky timing. If human resources are to become essential, we should be well placed. We may not have learned yet how to mobilize them, but human talents – an appreciation of fine quality, finished work, an abhorrence of waste – are some of the essential requirements of industry. We in Europe should have a better chance than others of succeeding, though places as diverse as Japan, with its consensus outlook, and California, with its blend of super-individualism and hyper-hedonism, are succeeding, despite their quite opposite cultures.

Fortunately some European companies are learning to mobilize their people. And the lessons to be drawn from Europe's competitive clashes with Japan and California are very much in line with the teachings of *In Search of Excellence*. Your company can win if:

- It is constantly alert to what is happening in the marketplace, not just inside the company.

- It is flexible enough in its structures to ensure its rapid response and adaptation to change.

- It is organized so that individuals and groups can contribute their full potential.

Type 3 companies whether in Japan, the United States or Europe, have many traits in common:

- They ensure that all employees feel the competitive pressures from the marketplace – the expectations of the customer. The market should penetrate into the shop floor.

- They create a sense of shared responsibility. The company's success is their group project.

- They operate with adaptable, flexible structures, which can be changed rapidly, which are action-oriented, and whose 'weight' is as light as possible. This helps create two key elements of a successful company – quickness and quality. This approach grows out of the Total

Quality Control System (TQCS) developed by the Americans and the Japanese.

- They ensure that every employee feels he has a useful and intelligent job. They achieve this by seeking out and eliminating non-productive jobs, forms of cancer inside industrial companies – especially large ones – whose stupidity or uselessness destroy workers' spirits.

- They regularly call upon the employees for ideas and suggestions, using two channels of communication: one for the improvement of daily work (such as quality circles), and the other drawing on the entire workforce for participation, and then better implementation of the company's strategy at all levels (for example, installing 'guidance circles' at the middle-management level).

- They provide dynamic management of the company's men and women, with special attention to the three groups essential for the company's future: the young (tomorrow's potential), the most senior (for their experience) and the future managers (those who will have long-term careers at the company).

- They develop management systems and training programmes to assure maximum decentralization and the cohesion of all parts of the organization.

Part I

WORKING TOGETHER WITHIN THE COMPANY

1 Better than forecasts: the four-speed plan

In 1982 Nippon Electric Co. (NEC) sent 150 employees around the world in search of the most promising technological innovations. In that same year another 5000 of NEC's total 35 000 employees travelled abroad. Also in 1982 the French company Lesieur inaugurated a policy of collaboration with small and medium-sized companies. The aim of the policy participation in the industrial development of innovation originating outside Lesieur, thereby feeding its own research and development.

In California at Hewlett-Packard's two management methods of great simplicity provide constant interchange among employees and a free flow of information – the open door system and MBWA (management by walking about). The open door policy requires managers literally to keep their doors open so as to be accessible when needed – and without excessive protocol. MBWA keeps managers in touch with employees. At least once a day all managers must leave their offices and seek out their subordinates for informal encounters.

NEC, Lesieur and Hewlett-Packard illustrate three initiatives, unrelated yet with similar objectives – to open up the company; to establish a better relation with the world; to liberate the company from the inside, breaking down the barriers, the fiefdoms, the walls of silence; to mobilize human talents.

It is nothing short of suicidal to adopt such attitudes as 'We are the best', 'Our engineers are the best', 'We rely on ourselves', or 'The only good technologies and products are ours'. These are Maginot Line attitudes – the false sense of security that makes you think you are shielded from problems. The successful companies are those that allow the perception of risk to penetrate to the shop floor, and these same companies are the ones that know how to make their culture evolve with reality, producing a level of effectiveness better than that of companies which close themselves up and try to make a corporate culture work for them even if it is outdated.

There are many ways to achieve this dual opening towards the outside and towards the inside:

- A participative planning policy.

- Maximum cross-fertilization, which comes from such mechanisms as bringing quality circles together or Mitsubishi's soft sciences groups.

- Regular visits to leading companies (Hewlett-Packard, Majorette) and to leading countries (Japan, the United States).

- A reporting system that requires each employee who has outside contacts with suppliers, customers or colleagues in competitive companies to share all information that might be helpful.

One of the most effective approaches seems to be the system we call 'the four-speed plan', developed by SRI International in Palo Alto, California. It is based on the obvious fact that conventional forecasting has been rendered unreliable by great social and political upheavals of the past twenty years. In 1900 the United States and Argentina were equals in gross national product, and seemed to hold equal promise for development. In 1965 the OECD classified Japan as an under-developed country, and in 1975 the Shah of Iran was taken seriously when he announced that Iran would be one of the great industrial powers by the end of the century. But as the French writer Alphonse Allais said once, 'The garbage cans of history are full of long-term trends'.

Economic forecasting today is not totally discredited, but

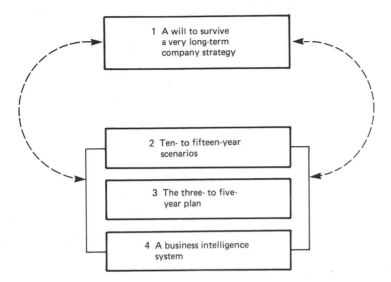

Figure 1.1   The 'four-speed' system

it has been put in its place as an intellectual exercise for developing plausible hypotheses; and since forcasting fell from grace, managers have been in a state of shock. They are forced to manage day-to-day while pretending to know where they are going, and to make ridiculous prognostications ('I see the light at the end of the tunnel') that are quickly proved wrong. They live in fear of being accused of incompetence if they admit they cannot foresee the future.

SRI's four-speed plan' (Figure 1.1) contends, however, that uncertainty offers an opportunity for those who know how to use it. In our unpredictable times the most optimistic, imaginative and enthusiastic among us will recognize the opportunities while the timid will see only threats, and the blind will see nothing at all.

1   The will to survive a very long term project

In these turbulent and aggressive times no company that lacks the profound desire to survive will be able to. The will is usually expressed as a mission ('To be the leader...', 'To contribute to the development...', 'To gain a share of the market . . .') or as an ethical position (principles or grand goals). Sun Tzu said, 'He who has no objective runs no risk of attaining it'. This applies to companies, perhaps with the postscript: 'No objective, no future'. Yet it is surprising how few companies have this outlook, or how few top management teams make the effort to define a mission and get the employees behind it.

2   The ten- to fifteen-year scenario

Scenarios provide an opportunity to analyse the key social, economic, political and technological factors affecting a company's future. The mere exercise forces one to understand the business environment better.

Scenarios should be concerned with the risks of the future, and rather than minimize the risks, the scenario should focus on ways to confront and overcome the dangers they present. This concentration on risks can help mobilize management.

Finally, scenarios are like moving pictures of the business context, not future snapshots of a company's assets (cash, products, personnel in x years). They do not consist of the separate views of the controller, the research and development director, the marketing vice-president, the personnel man and the manufacturing director, but a common approach, worked out by a group, covering several possible futures, so that whichever comes to pass, the company has the best chance of staying on track towards its objectives.

3   The three- to five-year plan

Scenarios are, by definition, stories of what *might* happen. They can be a useful tool for defining what strategies to adopt in the medium term, for which period forecasting and analysis have a role to play. Remember that plans should not be carved in stone. Plans should clarify and quantify what you want to do in the coming two or three years, and provide a context for next year's budget (rather than looking backwards and prolonging the past). It is less a question of predicting the future than of adopting a set of decisions to move towards an objective while staying flexible enough

to adopt any of the scenarios (worst case, best case or other options).
This plan should mobilize the people who will participate in making it a reality. It is an essential tool for information and dialogue for the entire company.

4   A business intelligence system

Trying to read signals from the marketplace can be risky, yet it is possible, with effort, to look into the future. This is as true for the company itself internally as for changes in the social, economic, political and technological environment. Unfortunately, great skill is required to interpret these signals because of a basic law: they are inversely proportional to the freedom of action a company will have in responding to the changes they indicate. A weak signal means an early stage of a coming trend, and time to adjust to it. A strong signals means you may have no choice but to follow. If the US car industry had understood the weak signals in 1960 from MITI, which announced Japan's ambitions for the next twenty years, Detroit could have coped better with the invasion. But few took notice.

Here are the main components of a business intelligence system (BIS):

- A scanning system to pick up all signals – not just those from your industry. The steel industry today could be sending out signals that tomorrow will interest the agricultural industry. 'Everything is related to everything else', notes SRI.

- Resources such as access to data banks are needed, as is a senior team of information-gatherers to attend conferences and seminars, to visit the leading companies, to read the journals and books being published, and to synthesize their observations, which can be applied for the benefit of the company.

- Proper training for all personnel in the filing of regular and *ad hoc* reports on all they have observed is required.

This is especially important for those who will work outside, at postings abroad, at seminars and in contact with customers. Others of course must be available internally to process this information in digestible form for management.

A **BIS** also needs a separate monitoring system to track developments that interest the company directly, such as materials or robotics.

These four elements – a long-term mission, the long- and medium-term plans and a business information system – will all help cope with the uncertainties of the future. The interaction of all four elements is where the payoff comes. The scenarios are the backdrop for all present and future actions of the company, and help guide the planning process, while the BIS indicates towards which scenario the company is moving, and whether it might be one not yet dreamed up by the scenario team.

Unfortunately some companies that use the four-speed approach bring only top management into the process. Yet all personnel would benefit from the opening it provides towards the outside and the inside of the company.

Seneca tells us, 'There are no favourable winds for those who have no port to go to'. But all the company's men and women, better educated and better informed nowadays, are encouraged to live responsible lives, not just as cogs in a machine, executing mechanical procedures hemmed in by rigid partitions. What better way to limit their capacity for judgement, reflection, imagination, crossfertilization and suggestion could there be than keeping them in ignorance of everything happening outside the company and even inside, in departments that don't directly concern them? This kind of backward attitude towards employees exemplifies the 'industrial sins' identified by the Japanese: re-inventing what has already been done elsewhere, developing products that have no market, and using only the intelligence of the managers, thereby squandering 99 per cent of the company's potential brainpower.

All components of the four-speed approach are straight-foward and simple to implement, except the definition of the company's mission. That must be tailored to the company's unique personality.

How to approach a mission definition

Here is an example of how one French oil company began the process.

Every company, by its very existence, possesses a charter that defines its grand design, its reason for being and its fundamental objectives, both economic and human. More often than not this charter is implicit, not written. It has been developed little by little, during the life of the enterprise, and is a combination of its economic aims, its technological prowess and its approach to human relations.

The difficulties our economy is experiencing today make it necessary for the links between the company and its employees to be strengthened. New and better methods of communication are needed to allow the employees' aspirations to be defined and taken into account. What has previously been implicit must therefore now be spelled out to draw all employees into the mission, which must be swept along on a wave of commitment. Does this wave exist?

A mission is merely the laying out of a design for this commitment. It must reflect reality and the future. It can be expressed in a few propositions that must share certain characteristics. It must:

- Liberate energies, mobilize, unite, satisfy, be reasonable, realistic, fair, ambitious and general but not too general; it must fit the company's potential; and it must be consistent.

- Go beyond the horizon of what can be planned.

- Speak to the needs of the employees.

- Appeal to the irrational in all of us; it is an adventure, a challenge.

- Build on the sociological foundation of the company.

- Be personified in one or several of the company's leaders.

- Have an outside adversary such as the marketplace or domestic and international competition.

To define the mission, certain facts can be set down in speeches or official declarations. To reach beyond today's problems, however, it must attempt to focus on the common denominator that will tie together short-term objectives over a period of several years.

The strategic aims should have implications for development. For example, if the company wants to become international, it must acquire an international outlook.

Once the objectives are listed, they must be checked to confirm that they match the company's culture. This kind of analysis can begin with a study of presentations and speeches being delivered in the company. But the analysis can be long and difficult. It is certainly more straightforward to identify some of the basic foundations of the corporate culture in several areas, such as:

- Technique: achievements and knowhow, quality, performance and new technology.

- Specific areas: energy, health (hygiene, veterinary industries, biotechnology), scientific and technical research, chemicals.

- Innovation: *National themes:* public service (energy independence, etc.), industrial leadership, regional involvement. *International themes:* negotiations, representation through diplomatic missions, initiatives in collaboration with Third World countries.

- The American market.

- The marketplace: competition, suppliers, customers.

- Company image: its people.

With the list complete, the propositions, under different labels, must be tested on representative samples.

This example may not be a perfect plan for defining every company's mission, but it helps show the way. Most of all it helps explain the methods. The different approaches of companies such as Hewlett-Packard (four principles and seven objectives of the Hewlett-Packard way) and Lafarge Coppée (specifying the managers' common values), indicate how important it can be to tailor the programme to the individual company. The needs are as follows:

1   In order to mobilize and unite the personnel the company's mission must encompass more than economic ambitions. Conquest of markets, or attaining leadership of an industry, can be inspirational, but only for the managers – especially for those in sales and marketing. Even though everyone realizes that commercial success is vital, not everyone in the company will extend himself to achieve it, certainly not in cases where the job is too isolated from that ambition.

If an economic aim is to be part of the mission, that alone should not be expected to rally the workforce. Other goals should enrich the mission, such as:

The human dimension

● The opportunity for rapid advancement.

● The development of all employees through training.

● A guarantee of constant innovation.

● The attraction of a rounded system of compensation: salary plus other perks and advantages.

A technological goal

● The company's processes should be in the vanguard of technological progress.

● The company should lead in robotics applications, for example.

A financial goal

● The company should aim, for example, to be profitable enough to finance its investment needs and to attract outside shareholders.

A good citizenship goal

- To help create jobs.
- To have an image of leadership in socio-economic management.
- To help promote innovation.

2 If one wishes to mobilize and unite, one cannot impose a mission from above. It must be a shared programme, designed by the people who will have to live with it, otherwise it loses all impact. Of course, if it is conceived by the top management, and written by the finest word-smith, it would perhaps make a more elegant statement. But elegance does not rally troops to battle. Actually the process of developing the mission is as important as the result.

3 Ambitions and goals are often abstract. The informa-tion glut and inflated rhetoric rob them of importance. Ambitions are credible only if the policies to achieve them and the priorities for action are clearly set. If goals are to be debated inside the company, the assign-ment of priorities can be decided in small groups employed to fix targets for such things as employment, diversification or adoption of new technology.

4 Finally, a company is a 'collective' that needs its own code of conduct, its own morality and its own values, which must be understood and recognized by all. Draw-ing up the code and values requires a review of company history, its specialities and its culture, and a description of how they should evolve in the future.

Lafarge Coppée found the answer by undertaking a long process to unite its managers under a single doctrine. This provides a consistent oulook through future generations of managers, ensuring a continuity in the company's diversification of technology and geographical decentralization.

The code of values is the law, in the monastic sense of the term – the kind of law that all communities of people must have when they set off on an adventure. The better the code, and the better its acceptance, the less need for regulation.

2 Better than management: 'reactivity'

Travellers passing through the duty-free shops of Singapore, Hong Kong, Taipei, Tokyo and Bahrain have noticed that the technical and commercial imagination in Asia has produced successive waves of products, each more fascinating than the last. Companies such as Casio and Toshiba have launched a creative assault on the consumer with a wide range of electronic games, organs and miniature synthesizers, and musical microcomputers that can wake you in the morning. On each visit the Western visitor discovers in these gigantic bazaars new gadgets to captivate him. And he buys them.

If it were only a matter of these gadgets, the West would having nothing to be concerned about. But the Asians' ability to sense the smallest change in consumer taste, and to satisfy it with a flow of new products, reveals a strength that many Western companies have no conception of. This ability to adapt quickly is just as impressive in other industrial sectors. Japanese industry, as in Silicon Valley, turns this market sensitivity into one of its main assets. The product cycle – from perception of need, to product development, to manufacture, to delivery to the customer – is reduced to a minimum. Indeed, depending on the type of product, the cycle is often cut by more than half. What would take a Western company two to five years might take a Japanese company six months to two years. There is nothing mysterious or secret about this ability to shorten the cycle. It is due to the special attention devoted to a close linkage of the phases of the cycle, coupled with a systematic openness to the suggestions of all who can contribute ideas. We have found no word to describe this combination, which we observed in Japan and California. We have therefore applied the word 'reactivity', which implies flexibility, speed and responsiveness.

Organizing for fast response

It is not easy to describe these qualities, but at least we can point out their main characteristics – those that will oblige us to make the most change in our way of thinking and acting. The concept requires a definition of biological rather than logical structures, and a view of work in terms of 'mission to accept' rather than 'task to accomplish'.

Figure 2.1 describes the cycle of a company's reaction to changed market needs. Here is a full explanation.

STEP 1: Recognition of new market need

The customer is king; it is he who must be satisfied. It is he who usually suggests, by his acceptance, rejection, criticism or way of using it, how a product should evolve; he is often the best person to conceptualize the next product. Engineers may develop the means, but customers show the way. Thus salespeople are crucial information-gatherers, who must be trained to listen to customers rather than learn 'the ten secrets of better selling'. Salespeople must learn to face criticism with humility rather than with the arrogance reflected in such phrases as, 'Our products are better than Brand X'. In addition, salespeople must be taught a team mentality, so that leads and tips are quickly exchanged – in a sales organization 'each man for himself' is a recipe for failure.

Indeed interpreting customers' reactions is so crucial that salespeople alone are sometimes not entrusted with the task. At Matsushita, for example, they are backed by a team of 'quality reporters', whose job is to get beyond point-of-sale reactions and collect all information that might help the company understand how customers use, appreciate or criticize

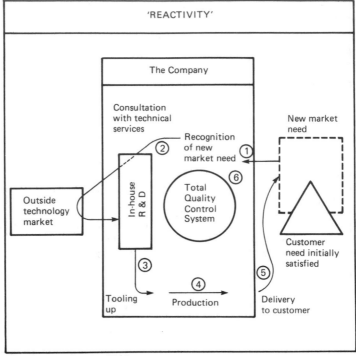

Source: Eurequip, Hervé Sérieyx

Figure 2.1   'Reactivity'

the product they have bought. All this data is analysed daily.
Almost daily the company adds new features, produces new
models, new packaging, and identifies new uses. From one
minor change to another, eventually a new product is born.

STEP 2: Consultation with technical services

The marketing services in Japan and Silicon Valley have direct
lines into the technical services to pass on their suggestions
– whether it be only an evolutionary change or a leap in
technology. Research and development might be asked to
apply off-the-shelf technology to enhance a product, or a
sort of 'creativity pool' can be tapped. At Mitsubishi, for
example, a 'soft sciences group' is made up of men and women

from a variety of jobs in the company. They meet once a month and they serve in the group for one or two years. At their monthly meetings they are asked to respond to two types of question:

- New expectations have been identified among our customers. 'How would you satisfy them?'
- R&D has just come up with some new technologies. 'What marketable applications can you suggest?'

For Japanese and Silicon Valley companies one of the capital sins is to re-invent the wheel. If the means exist elsewhere, somehow they must be appropriated. Mitsubishi, Toshiba and NEC all invest heavily in permanent monitoring of the technology market. Through acquisition of patents, by licence or franchise deals, by absorbing small companies, even by methods approaching industrial espionage, they stay abreast of the state of the art. When the customer's needs change, the company is thus able to find the best answer, even if in-house R&D or the 'creative pool' of the company cannot immediately produce a solution. The main thing is to respond rapidly.

STEPS 3 AND 4: Tooling up and production

Here also response time must be shortened. A new or modified product requires machinery and changes in the production process. The important role of quality circles in this process is recognized in Europe. In these two steps, where it is so easy to lose time, the Japanese and Californians are expert at mobilizing their people at all levels, tapping their critical spirit, their suggestions and the intelligent interpretation of their experience. It is especially in these steps that Japan wins the battle of fast reaction.

STEP 5: Delivery to customer

The big Japanese companies are so committed to the total quality concept that the sales network goes into intensive training as soon as a new product is decided upon. After-sales service people interact immediately with the sales force and product design team to propose changes in the way the product might be used, the colour scheme and other details. When the product arrives at the end of the chain, the sales department is intimately familiar with it. Salespeople are charged up to sell it, and their sales pitch is already perfected.

STEP 6: Total quality control

Many companies will say they recognize the importance of maintaining a total quality system, but for most managers it is only one of many systems in place. In Japan, however, the Total Quality Control System (TQCS) actually monitors all the other management systems in the company. The reason is that in Japan 'quality' means 'quality of responsiveness to the customer', and all activities of the company are co-ordinated to serve that aim. It is this regard for quality, plus the constant effort to shorten lead times, that will set the pace for the reactivity process.

Simply put, reactivity works best when companies call on the combined brainpower of their employees. These companies respond faster than their competition to the challenges of new technologies and the challenges of the marketplace.

In the area of new technology problems such as enormous waste or poor execution of the new product cycle can result if the company's culture is not receptive. Prof. Richard Goodman of the University of California at Los Angeles says that of 100 new product ideas floated in US companies, only thirty become serious contenders for development, only eight make it to market, and only one becomes commercially successful. This helps explain why Type 3 companies place such emphasis on the management of technological development.

A technological innovation has a better chance to survive the project stage if it is in phase with the company objectives, market orientation and competitors' technological progress. All this assumes that the research and development teams are aware of the company's objectives (which is not always the case) and the changes in the marketplace (which is even rarer). The researchers must not be isolated in design bureaux and laboratories. They run the risk of developing brilliant products that no one wants or re-inventing the products of competitors – two errors that can cost dearly in time, money and energy.

A climate for innovation can be created if several basic attitudes are adopted. A team of dedicated researchers must be recruited, and staff turnover among its members kept to a minimum. But R&D should have no monopoly of innovation: all functions of the company must be concerned with it. Top management must be understanding about the vagaries of innovation. More important, managment needs to show understanding of the risk an employee assumes when he takes on an innovative project, and the efforts of the researcher and the project managers should be compensated independently of the project's success or failure.

One cautionary note: innovations can cause downstream dislocations in such functions as production and marketing. It is top management's job to co-ordinate departments of the company as the innovation becomes a reality.

As we have implied already, there is no innovation possible in a company that is not open in spirit. There are three kinds of openness that must be achieved to let in the fresh air of creativity: in technology the staff needs data banks, attendance at scientific and technical conferences, and visits to pace-setting companies; in the marketplace the sales team should be visiting customers, suppliers and countries where users of the product are most sophisticated; and in terms of mentality managers and others should be using established techniques – brainstorming, synectics, soft sciences groups, etc. – to stimulate creativity.

Innovation cannot be managed on a shoestring: resources are required, and care must be taken to choose projects that have a reasonable chance to succeed. Two key decisions can make the difference.

The choice of product champion is the more crucial. He or she must be a manager of high quality – a leader, motivator and an interpreter who has a good track record. Secondly, adequate financing must be provided to ensure a good start, for underfunded projects are the ones that end up costing the most. If management is careless about thost two points, the company is better off saving itself a lot of time and money by opting out of the game altogether.

A good example of how to do it is the method employed at Tandem. A massive emphasis on communication and commitment ensures a broad awareness of the company's goals, which helps keep the flow of ideas in phase. Tandem's employees gather ideas from the marketplace, from customers, and even from competitors. A product manager is put in charge, and each new idea is put to the product planning group, which meets once a quarter to choose the most marketable proposals.

If the idea is approved, the product manager takes the project through the following four-part sequence: calculation of production plans, drawing up of specifications, production start-up, and test and quality control. Finally, the product is launched.

The product manager pilots his project from idea to marketplace not by top–down directives but by consensus, while preparing the company's infrastructure to support the launch. He delegates much of the responsibility both to bring in employees down the pyramid and to draw on the competence of people at the level at which the problems occur.

Tandem claims great benefits from the system. All ideas that survive the product planning group make it to market, and the ideas that die along the way never take up more than two or three months of a product manager's time. The entire cycle, from idea to marketplace, never takes more than two years.

Reactivity: combating National Workshops and the 'phantom factory'

After the French revolution of 1848 workplaces were set up in Paris and several provincial cities as a job-creation measure. Little by little the original vision faded, and eventually these National Workshops became a symbol of those ridiculous programmes that employ people just to keep them busy. The ultimate example was to have men digging holes and filling them in again. We laugh at this today, but in fact we have our own versions of National Workshops in many companies, especially in the big firms.

We are not pleading for excessive pressure for productivity and cutbacks in personnel. In fact we want to argue for the opposite: that it is a crime to force intelligent employees to perform useless, unproductive tasks, and to try to tell the workers such jobs are worthwhile. It is even more serious when managers deceive themselves into believing this kind of manpower utilization makes sense.

Too many companies are keeping 20 to 30 per cent of their workers occupied with work devoted to adding 'value' that has no market. What contempt this shows for the intelligence of the workers! We are a long way from the effectiveness of companies such as Nissan and Tandem. Tandem is one of Silicon Valley's most spectacular success stories. How does it do it? Every job – the telephonist's, the canteen manager's, the marketing manager's – is designed as a challenge.

What is called for is an organization of complementary challenges. This requires a huge effort on the part of management, which must have an intimate knowledge of the men and women who take up the challenges. Tandem does it, and at Nissan an aggressive advertising campaign says the company has such a high regard for its personnel that jobs requiring the most intelligence are reserved for its workers – tasks that the most sophisticated robots could not execute, tasks that call for judgement of a high quality. Nissan watches out for unproductive jobs, not unproductive people, seeking to ensure that each employee has a job that is enriching, full of growth potential and indispensable.

The Nissan viewpoint can be expressed in another way: in a company of 1000 employees that makes 1000 products there is no point hunting down the unproductive employees so that 600 workers could produce 1000 products. But in seeking out the counterproductive jobs or practices in the company, and making sure that each worker has a truly contributory role, those same 1000 people might well be able to produce 2000 products. If the workers really feel that their

jobs have some purpose, their commitment is secured. It is one of management's biggest responsibilities.
Something very close to that was needed in Dijon, as François Perrin-Pelletier described it:

> In our Dijon plant three days passed from the moment a steel rod entered the door till it exited in the form of a finished product. In fact, however, the rod was actually being worked only 11 minutes. Our engineers set about trying to reduce the three-day timespan. They worked with great intelligence and effort. But no one focused on the real opportunity: to reduce the time during which the rod was being guarded, stored, conditioned – all the intermediary steps. No one mobilized the staff to produce that intangible added value. This is the phantom 'company within a company' – the misuse of resources, human or material, that adds to the cost of the output.

It can be a shock to discover just how much 'phantom' activity takes place in a company. For example, the down-time rate on key equipment might be too high, but tacitly accepted by shop-floor supervisors; and the slow delivery of materials from suppliers, might also be considered 'acceptable' by personnel, as might the level of quality tolerated or the build-up of inventories – there is no shortage of things that feed the phantom. One recent study of 127 companies by the French Industry Ministry indicated that 10 per cent is added to production costs by rejected production, repairs, reimbursement for damaged output, etc.

It is a question of attitude. Examining the phantom enter-prise can be frightening, but it can also be regarded as a golden opportunity to make changes for the better. Truly reorganizing production so that all resources are channelled into adding value will give a solid boost to performance.

Companies intent on tracking down the phantom have identified five 'zeros' that must be achieved:

Zero downtime assumes that it better to have no breakdowns than to have an excellent team of repairmen. Breakdowns cause bottlenecks, interrupt continuity, halt the flow of goods upstream and downstream, swell intermediate stocks, and cause a build-up of work in progress.

Zero delay can cover such things as set-up times, making payments, mail delivery, the implementation of decisions. Delays of all kinds build up the work-in-progress load and immobilize resources.

Zero defect assumes that it is better to manufacture without defect in the first place than to have a rigorous quality-control system at the end of the line. It is a waste either way: declaring a product defective or declaring it acceptable. In a well run company each worker is trained to be his own quality controller. Defects can be caught at the component or sub-assembly stage. In this way a defect might mean a cost of 10, but at the end of the line it would mean a cost of 100 – and a customer's return might cost 1000.

Zero inventory comes nearer reality when the three previous zeros are part of the programme. But the Toyota method of *kanban* or 'just in time' inventory control can squeeze inventory costs further. Quality guarantees can be imposed on suppliers to ease the upstream costs and firm up delivery. Nissan has made the system work, and hundreds of US companies have borrowed or adopted it.

Zero paper is a tough objective for European companies, where there is a love of filling out forms, procedures and memos. This sets in motion a great flood of paper. Often new forms do not replace old ones, they are supplementary; and procedures are not 'biodegradable', they pile up on one another like sediment on the sea-bed. Our in-trays are clogged daily with memos that must be read, dealt with, filed away, even though the sender probably wrote them to please himself. What a waste of time and energy! Administration must be subjected to the same scrutiny as the shop floor. Try asking yourself some of these questions. Is this form necessary? Are these copies necessary? Isn't this procedure a duplication of another? Does this really have to be filed?

Well-run companies are striving for the five zeros, and as they move towards that objective, they find that they can reassign resources. In the process they are 'starving the phantom', putting people to work at meaningful jobs, and improving the company's competitiveness. Everyone must join in. At the French company Lesieur the five-zero concept is the centrepiece of the effort to win the commitment of

employees. Everyone strives for the goals because everyone
will benefit from moving towards it.

Nissan, Tandem and many European companies have recognized that the employees also wanted the phantom eliminated.
The workers were rebelling against mindless, useless tasks.
The paradox of our time is that our people are becoming
better educated, better informed, more active in society as
responsible citizens, while spending eight hours a day
performing sterile, hopeless tasks, wasting their lives to earn
a living.

In no way should Japan become our guiding light, but
we can learn certain lessons from Japan's experience. When
a society is struggling to raise the level of its culture, industrial
life must keep pace. Rather than digging holes only to fill
them in, workers should be building cathedrals.

Reactivity and fluid structures

Many companies, large and small, suffer from rigid organizational structures that resist change. This is nothing new. We
have been brought up to think within an established framework. From childhood our educational system teaches us
that authority means separation, distance creates respect, and
acquired information confers power upon people who apply
it in discrete units and ensure the organization's success.
Creatures of the Taylor model, each of us withdraws little
by little into our territory, as a sense of possession takes
over the divisional management (*my* staff, *my* secretaries,
my services), conducting a kind of warfare to defend the
division's turf.

So the marketing director makes sure his counterpart from
R&D keeps his nose out of marketing affairs, manufacturing
feels the same about maintenance, and the whole company
becomes a patchwork of conflicting ambitions. Each department is more intent upon protecting its flanks than in contributing to the total performance of the company.

Type 3 companies get to grips with this catastrophic frag-
mentation by preventing everything and everyone contribut-

ing to the hardening of boundaries, the compartmentalization of company structures. Instead maximum flexibility is the goal. Little by little the old functional lines are erased, the complicated matrix organization fades away, and task forces, with objectives that are understood by all, are created. The message becomes loud and clear: territorial structures are out, mission-oriented structures are in.

Peters and Waterman are adamant, in their book *In Search of Excellence*, that flexibility is the essential element in management's ability to respond rapidly to competitive conditions. They summarized the characteristics of their 'excellent' companies in the following eight points:

1 *A bias for action*, for getting on with it. Even though these companies may be analytical in their approach to decision-making, they are not paralysed by that fact (as so many others seem to be). In many of these companies the standard operating procedure is 'Do it, fix it, try it'.

2 *Close to the customer*. These companies learn from the people they serve. They provide unparalleled quality, service and reliability – things that work and last.

3 *Autonomy and entrepreneurship*. The innovative companies foster many leaders and many innovators throughout the organization. They do not try to hold everyone on so short a rein that they cannot be creative. They encourage practical risk-taking, and support good tries. They follow Fletcher Byrom's ninth commandment: 'Make sure you generate a reasonable number of mistakes'.

4 *Productivity through people*. The excellent companies treat the rank and file as the root source of quality and productivity gain. They do not foster us/them labour attitudes or regard capital investment as the fundamental source of efficiency improvement.

5 *Hands-on, value-driven*. Thomas Watson, Jr, said that 'the basic philosophy of an organization has far more to do with its achievement than do technological or

economic resources, organizational structure, innovation and timing'.

6 *Stick to the knitting.* Robert W. Johnson, former Johnson & Johnson chairman, put it this way: 'Never acquire a business you don't know how to run'. While there are a few exceptions, the odds for excellent performance seem strongly to favour those companies that stay reasonably close to businesses they know.

7 *Simple form, lean staff.* As big as most of the companies we have looked at are, none when we looked at it were formally run with a matrix organization structure, and some which had tried that form had abandoned it. The underlying structural forms and systems in the excellent companies are elegantly simple.

8 *Simultaneous loose–tight properties.* The excellent companies are both centralized and decentralized. For the most part, as we have said, they have pushed autonomy down to the shop floor or product-development team. On the other hand, they are fanatic centralists around the few core values they hold dear.

3 Better than motivation: mobilization

Is the economic wineglass half full or half empty? Western industrialists today had best try to see it as half full. Falling into a pessimistic view of the world – with its fluctuating exchange rates, government controls, new competition from Asia – is a short cut to losing all the energy needed to stay in the race. The essential is to focus on the company's strength, not on the past, when a different company operated in a different environment. The source is all those elements of a company that are not yet mobilized. The one asset we have not begun to exploit in the West is the technical competence of employees; in view of the diversity of people available, it is fair to say we have not scratched the surface of their potential. A few years ago a senior executive of the French group Lesieur was on a visit to Japan. There he met one leading Japanese industrialist, who had this advice to offer:

> You European entrepreneurs are going to lose out to us. You will lose because defeat is already in your minds. You are thoroughly convinced that competitive companies are made up of people on top who think and people below who carry out instructions. Even those of you who sometimes say the opposite believe this. But we Japanese, who have been far more devoted to Taylorism than you, are now convinced that in a world of greater uncertainty, turbulence, aggressiveness, a company's chances of survival are so tenuous that all its resources must be used, down to the modest contributor... To you, management is the art of

37

conveying management's ideas down to the workers. Our approach is to engage the intelligence of all employees in the service of a specific mission. In short, the reverse of your method.

The Japanese industrialist was right. Common sense also should be enough to dictate that we must listen to others, to call on their creative forces, on their desire to contribute. These contributions should be sought by management and recognized for their real value, instead of restricting the company to management strengths alone. When Toyota can claim to have collected 570,000 ideas for progress from its personnel, and put 500,000 of these ideas to use, it is clear what a strategic advantage the company has over its competitors, many of whom have not invited their workers to contribute at all.

In 1980 about fifteen French executives toured the Pacific Basin to see what common features they could identify between the best managed companies of California and Japan. The most striking similarity to emerge was that companies on both sides of the Pacific were trying their best to develop a style that fitted in with their surrounding social and cultural environments.

Other travellers, and such books as William Ouchi's *Theory Z*, have confirmed our hypothesis: Japanese perform better if they work under Japanese-style management, and Californians work best under California-style management. The vague structures, the 'groupism' and consensus fulfil a Japanese need. Their organization may be incomprehensible to us, but the progressive decision-making of the *ringi* method, the concerted effort of the *nemawashi* method, the big rabbit-hutch offices where administrative staffs are jammed together, work for them. Similarly in California the exaggerated American individualism and hedonism is satisfied by relaxed, free-wheeling management, in which all the formal practices of an organization (order, reverence for hierarchy, etc.) are minimized to best exploit the specific virtues of Californian culture – taste for challenging the conventional, for super-performance and for constant creativity.

The story of the French Quality Circle Association shows how enthusiastic some French companies are for management styles that treat employees for what they are, not for what the company decides to take from them. The Association was founded in 1981 by a handful of supporters, and was soon packing conferences throughout the country on the methods for organizing QCs. By 1985 there were eighteen regional chapters, a magazine, and a board made up of the country's biggest companies. The Association now has the support of government and trade unions, and counts some 400 companies, or about 30 per cent of the French working population, among its members. The growth of the Association shows how the ability to remake the world of work has captured the imagination of French business.

Of course there is an overtone of naivety in this rediscovery of what are actually old methods. It is reminiscent of the story of the architect who wanted to bring some warmth and humanity to the concrete jungles that have been created as 'new towns' or mass housing projects in some parts of Europe. His aim was to add some structures with softer lines, perhaps articulated, to provide some shade and some colour. After a survey he determined that green was the preferred colour, and so, after a few tries, he was successful. He re-invented the tree.

Quality circles are the 'rediscovery of the tree'. Working life becomes natural again, much as it was before Taylorism made it so artificial. We are not talking about reverting to Rousseau's idealism creating a 1960s' 'happening' among employees, or rejecting all forms of industrial structure or organization of work. We are all too well trained by the civilization of technology to indulge in such excesses. It is merely a matter of mobilizing in the most natural way this potential wealth of energy and intelligence that our impoverished, mechanistic view of the world has led us to ignore and to scorn (or at the very least to sterilize).

Yet in implementing quality circles, there is a danger of failure if four pitfalls are not kept in mind:

Pitfall 1 The philosopher's stone was the alchemist's dream – a substance that would change metals into gold, and also cure all ills. The illusion is that quality circles will solve all problems, replace everything, transform poor products into good ones, bad organizations into effective ones and poorly trained employees into competent workers. Quality circles can only make good products and good organizations better, and properly trained workers more capable.

Pitfall 2   Getting things backward, and believing that the means is the end – that quality circles are created for the pleasure of creating them. Actually quality circles are useful only insofar as they serve their purpose: to revive the spirit of the enterprise. If the company is not prepared for the revolution, it is better off not going for this approach.

Pitfall 3   An excess of zeal can lead to efforts to accomplish too much too soon. Caution is important. Prepare the ground before planting. Try to find the natural harmonies of the group, free of the sterile structures within which people have developed their work habits. Preparation and deliberation are paramount. All necessary time must be taken to undo all that must be undone before creating each new quality circle.

Pitfall 4   Underestimation of the mobilization task can wreck the effort. The intelligence of all concerned must be engaged, including that of the supervisors and managers. Often a company sits unknowingly on an immense deposit of underutilized talent and imagination. Indeed what managers would accept suggestions from subordinates in a company where their own proposals are ignored, or where they are not consulted in the definition of strategy of their own departments, their division or their factory?

There can be no quality without circles of guidance – groups of managers who focus on specific procedures and methods of operating to resolve problems of strategy and management that affect their level. Some companies are beginning to benefit from this dual system of interlocking circles, in which company objectives are fed down into guidance circles, and a flow of ideas from the shop floor moves up into quality circles.

Is there a danger that we may create a workforce that becomes more and more demanding of its top management? Workers will be challenging the direction of the company with such questions as 'How are we doing?', 'What is our target?', 'Where will we be in five years' time?' Is it true that the company will be a less comfortable place for top management. What makes it a workable arrangement is the joint commitment to the corporate mission.

To be blunt, a company that is flying blind, that has no real direction or desire to work with its employees, would be heading for suicide if it set up a quality circles programme. It would be like a pressure cooker with the lid tightly fastened. Without an effort to harness and orientate this power, sooner or later bitterness and revolt set in. But when the programme is properly launched and managed, the company becomes bolder, more intense, more open and more competitive.

Our education system turns out first-class professionals in technology, in sales and marketing, in management. But until very recently, little attention has been paid to developing a sense of openness, the ability to listen and the need to avoid the one-man show.

We have of course not been able to cover all the elements that can make participation successful. Imagination and the individual touch will be necessary. But some idea of the range of components is provided by the results of one consultancy's study of ten high-performance companies that sought to draw upon their employees' contributions and to take account of their socio-cultural values. Table 3.1 may seem an oversimplification, but it may open some avenues for reflection.

It is fascinating to see how times change. Throughout the industrialized world, in all the well-run companies, the top–down know-all managers are beginning to give way to managers who know how to listen and provide cohesiveness of purpose, and who can manage groups. These are the managers who factor in the values of others, so that more force can be developed in the effort. The people in the company become the engine, not the brakes; they are managed as a resource, not viewed as a constraint; and the payoff is the improved competitiveness of the enterprise.

When a company has been managed traditionally for decades, it cannot be transformed overnight into a Type 3 enterprise.

Table 3.1
Elements in participation

Values	Themes	Management methods
Appreciation of a job well done	Quality, innovation	Total quality as a priority; quality circles
A taste for challenge	Competition	Challenge situations for teams
Rejection of waste	Sense of economizing	Quality circles, training for conservation
Design to work together	Participation	Project teams, task forces, quality circles
Differentiation	Self-realization	Networks of microcomputers, decentralization
Resentment of being manipulated	Sensitivity	Clear objectives, guidance circles, MBWA

The danger is that enthusiasm for experimentation may get out of hand and hamper day-to-day operations. Many executives have ignored these cautionary notes to their regret. Their managers have been shocked to see their jobs made more difficult – ordinary responsibilities plus the orders to make the system change, and of course without the necessary resources.

This situation creates a dysfunction and a kind of dual dissatisfaction. First of all, top management's call for change has no effect, so the company becomes schizophrenic: one personality has been proclaimed but another – the old one – lives on. The gap between the two undermines the credibility of top management in the eyes of employees. Adding to the problem, the dual dissatisfactions collide: senior executives' perception is that its managers are not being effective in implementing change, and management is embittered by lack of sympathy for the real difficulties of implementation.

Management experts have long been aware of this divide between the strategic and the operational. One of the most brilliant analysts of organizational problems, Igor Ansoff, proposes a concept called integrative management, which links the great strategic options with their translations into action. Many executives have been obliged to shelve their ambitious plans for change because the need for better integration was poorly understood. Among the tools of integrative management the most important for implementing the components of the Type 3 enterprise is the management of human resources. Traditionally human resources management is made up of six functions, which are broken down into twenty sub-functions.

An effective human resources system, however it is organized, must fulfil the following functions:

- The smoother introduction of new employees into the company.

- 'Personal dynamics' – ensuring that employees devote part of their energies to the goals of the company.

- Progress – preparing employees for the new skills demanded by tomorrow's needs.

- Internal dialogue, on a permanent, construcive basis. The quality of this dialogue often helps determine the effectiveness of the company.

- Quality of work life, including as much security as possible, and a fair share in the fortunes of the enterprise. The company is a community confronting a risk, and employees should 'go to war' together.

- Image-building, in terms of a humane system of organization, so that the labour market has a clear understanding of the company's special qualities. Well managed, this helps attract the best people.

In the Book *In Search of Excellence* the authors note the growing importance of conveying this image so that campus recruitment at the best universities brings results.

Table 3.2 relates the six human resource functions to the

Table 3.2
Human resources management

Functions	Sub-functions
1 Introduction	Recruitment Welcome and orientation Assignment to first job
2 Personnel dynamics	Compensation Communication Encouragement Career development Mobility
3 Progress	Receptivity to employees' ideas Training Cross-fertilization Job enrichment
4 Dialogue	Internal collaboration Negotiation
5 Quality of work-life	Security Improved working conditions Employee benefits
6 Image	Labour market information Information for other target groups

twenty sub-functions. Each of these sub-functions could be examined in detail as a component of the Type 3 enterprise. But in the interest of brevity we will look closely at only a few.

Recruitment

Most companies hire personnel for specific jobs each time a need arises, which is the best way to create tomorrow's unemployed. The needs of a company evolve constantly, but a specific job exists only temporarily in a company's history.

To recruit a person with capabilities that are too limited therefore is to run the risk of discovering one day that the need for such a person has disappeared. This kind of recruitment is totally wrong for companies that intend to benefit from better use of their employees' intelligence and energies. Hiring should be done in waves of specified types of people to enrich the company with talents and competence that meet future needs. Employee qualifications must be defined of course, but so must background (technical, legal, commercial, literary) and qualities (ability to listen, to lead groups, drive and enthusiasm). These waves will become groups of people that will facilitate the spread of new ideas, of dynamism and of new attitudes inside the company.

Welcome and orientation

It is striking to note how many ten-year employees have virtually no knowledge of their firm, how it functions, or what their colleagues do. Yet how can a company hope to achieve the smooth development of a product – from conception to sale – if in this long chain of processes no one knows what is happening one link up or one link down? This problem has been solved in companies that know how to introduce employees into the firm. New recruits spend their first weeks learning about company objectives, its history and culture. When this kind of orientation is practised on waves of recruits, the effort takes the form of seminars. In companies where people are considered the factor that makes the difference between success and failure, it is not excessive to devote four to six weeks to such a welcoming programme. Lockheed Space and Missiles, for example, spreads orientation over a period of twelve weeks, alternating sessions between briefings and debriefings. This is the perfect time to explain the ideas of Type 3 companies.

Career development

We have lived through the dream of career planning. The 1970s saw a spate of elaborate programmes in which consultants analysed employees' competence and potential, and the present and future jobs in the company, and prophesied where shortfalls would occur. But so many new technologies got in the way of such studies that all the conclusions – technical, economic, and even political and sociological – were quickly obsolete. It often happens that poor performance or a rigid or technocractic system can lead management to take a *laissez faire* attitude towards hiring. This is regrettable. Perhaps it is too much to stay on top of the changes both in people and in the nature of jobs simultaneously, but it is possible to develop career paths that will prepare employees for the unpredictable future. The only certainty is that they will have to be flexible enough to live amid change and uncertainty.

A sub-division of dynamic career development is the preparation of future executives for the company. We are not saying that companies should be preparing an elite, that top-level academic training is worthless, or that the best institutions are short on quality students. We are only trying to say – to shout – that the teams needed at the top of companies must be more than technically competent. They must also be able to work with others, with passion, with humour, accepting uncertainty, risk and hard work, without internal jealousies. The ones who must be separated out are the loners, those who want to rule their departments without sharing, those who have not learned to work together.

Training

This is the sub-function that translates the great strategic thrusts into action. Everyone talks about it, but how many do it? Toshiba does, for one, spending 10 per cent of its total payroll on internal training. State-supported education trains people to face the vagaries of life, but industry has a more precise mission: to take people as they are, with their strengths and weaknesses, and give them the training they need to conceive, manufacture and sell products that customers will want, will buy and want again. This is what justifies a company's existence and enables it to survive. This is the obvious lesson from Japan, the master of world competitiveness.

Among the training packages needed in this sub-function is one from Lesieur called 'cursus', or course. This is a review of all the facts, themes and reflections the managers need to master to give the company its coherence and its dynamism. An example of cursus is given in our last chapter. Of course every company must tailor its own cursus to fit its own targets and history.

Cross-fertilization

This is an essential sub-function for the management of human resources. The more a company wishes to be the master of its future, the more it must understand that younger generations can learn from the experience of olders ones. Many American companies are asking their retiring employees to spend their last few months writing their memoirs, so to speak. The outgoing employees review their careers, listing the things they feel they contributed to the company, and offering their advice to those who might join the company.

Job enrichment

Owing to the unfortunate chasm separating managers and workers, we are taught to think in terms of 'job enrichment' for the former, but of 'improved working conditions' for the latter.

For managers, there is often an ambiguity that skews the entire question of relations within a hierarchy. Dr Marcel Filiu, one of the founders of a consultancy called Eurequip, has described it in terms so precise and so strong, that his words are worth quoting:

Delegation usually means top down – from the superior to the subordinate. There seems to be an error here that shows either a misunderstanding of history or a misunderstanding of the democratic system we live in. Each person who enters the labour market has been conditioned by society to take on all facets of his role as a human being. If he is required to participate in a group, he has all the rights of a citizen. Most notably, he has the right to be treated as an equal of his fellow man.

Yet what is really going on? For the sake of direction and coherence, the responsibility for the group must be assumed by one person. All subordinates surrender certain rights, such as bad temper, oversensitivity, self-determination, setting of certain priorities. The condition is that the transfer of rights be handled with respect by the higher authority, and that such benefits as remuneration and gratification accrue from the relationship. Agreeing to suppress his sense of indignation, for example, the employee asks in return that no methods be used that would cause indignation. There is yet another form of delegation that could be called horizontal: when one member of a group assumes a function, the others tend to avoid taking on the same role, by economic agreement.

This is important for any manager who wishes to determine the individual worth of each individual who makes up the group. It is wise to bear in mind that managers tend to see their employees through the somewhat distorted prism of a balanced group. This poor understanding of the psychological reality of delegation, and the way the dominant role obliterates part of the personality of the person playing the role, seem to us to be two factors that account for the malaise – the revolt – among many executives today.

Developing a better system of delegating, one that would gradually re-establish equality in the relation, guaranteeing people a way of being subordinates while conserving their freedom of expression and without their becoming inferiors – this is the direction we must move in if we are to benefit from the intelligence available and therefore be competitive in the marketplace.

Actually more progress has been made in job enrichment for workers than for managers, because it is easier to accomplish at the lower levels. Very few companies have been able to design a better system for organizing the work of their managers, but for the workers it was absolutely essential to make improvements in the degree of responsibility with which they were entrusted. There have been some original schemes, such as the 'decentralized credits' (see p. 88) of the Lesieur group. To make their stated aims more credible, Lesieur allocated to each worker the equivalent of about £50, which the worker could use as he pleased – either individually or with co-workers – to finance any improvements he wished in the working environment to make the job more interesting or more comfortable. The programme resulted in some 3000 innovations or improvements.

Internal collaboration

This is obviously one of the most effective systems for translating policy into routine operations. Japanese companies are adamant about the need to interlock various groups to ensure good communications. In designing their flow of information through the company they link several meetings so that a common purpose is established. Management committee, divisions, departments, product groups, personnel committees, sales committees, buyers' committees must be deliberately interrelated. A company cannot be reduced to a 'mechanical' assembly of pulleys, wheels and cogs, as traditional organization charts suggest. It is a network of multiple means of communication, with many crossovers in the network. Opportunities for information exchange, reflection and proposals for improvements must be planned. Such committees should ensure:

● That everything that is obviously necessary actually exists in the company.

● That meetings are well run, with an agenda, a leader, a three-hour maximum duration and a summary of accomplishments.

● That committees duplicating the work of other committees, or committees that are useless for other reasons, are swiftly disbanded.

A good starting point is to draw a diagram of the interconnections already in place. This reveals strengths and weaknesses, serves as a critical analysis of the effort to build a common mission in the company, and helps to identify gaps in the network that are impeding the implementation of policy.

If all the elements of the Type 3 company we have explored and explained are realized, and all the potential and energies

are engaged, the company will surely become more competitive. The record speaks for itself: companies using this model
are among the best performers – in Japan, in the United
States and in Europe.

Part II

WORKING TOGETHER OUTSIDE THE COMPANY

4 A tale of three companies

The Mitsui story: how to turn a constraint into a strength

On 21 October 1945 the top managers of the Mitsui group were called together in the great conference hall of the Mitsui club in Tokyo to hear the US occupation authorities order the company to be dissolved, and its individual companies to operate on their own. All the big commercial and industrial groups of the time – the *zaibatsu,* as Mitsui, Mitsubishi, Sumitomo, Yasuda and others were called – were dismantled. The liquidation commission confiscated all the shares controlled by the *zaibatsu.* Members of the controlling families had no choice but to accept a reduction in their means as all their assets were taken over. Surprisingly, in most cases the owners and managers remained calm in accepting this terrible constraint.

The case of Mitsui is particularly interesting. A special restriction was imposed on more than 100 Mitsui veterans, forbidding them to create a new company. The restriction also covered shareholdings, direct and indirect. Although the *zaibatsu* disappeared, and the individual companies went off on their own, their managers gradually established informal contact again. It was thus that by 1950, just five years after the break-up, twenty-seven Mitsui directors decided that it would be useful to meet regularly over a working lunch on Mondays. The Monday Club was born, with the dual objective of organizing strategies for cross-holdings and to define the usage of the name Mitsui. The most important members of the new 'family' of managers were brought together in the club.

Five years later, in 1955, the presidents of the twelve largest companies decided to create the Group of Volunteers to help develop alliances and mergers. The Group became known as the Second Thursday of the Month Club, and it still meets – not to make big decisions but to guide policy and inter-company relations. Today the club includes twenty-four members, led by Mitsui Bank, Mitsui & Co., and Mitsui Real Estate Development, the most influential. A committee of directors was created to look after public relations and to co-ordinate the development of the image of member companies. Leading companies such as Toshiba and Toyota have joined the family, and they regularly take part in the effort to weave the companies together. Today the Mitsui family unites sixty-two first-rank companies, most of which control other companies. The sixty-two firms are in fact linked directly through their presidents and indirectly with about 2000 related companies (see Figure 4.1).

Before the war the economic significance of the *zaibatsu* was enormous. The four main *zaibatsu*, or groups linked by capital, represented 24 per cent of all capital invested in Japanese companies. Mitsui, the largest of them, accounted for 10 per cent by itself. Today the sixty-two main Mitsui companies employ 240 000 people, and the 2000 companies under them fall into four broad categories:

- Those financed and controlled directly by Mitsui Bank.

- Those in which Mitsui Bank or Mitsui & Co. hold large shareholdings.

- Those that trade heavily within the group (but have little or no financial ties).

- Lastly, those linked through various other ways to several companies in the group.

The central policy of the group, set forth by the clubs, applies to all member companies.

Company	N	G	K
Daicel Chemical Industries Ltd		•	•
Denki Kagaku Kogyo Kabushiki Kaisha		•	•
Fuji Kisen Kaisha Ltd		•	
Fujikura Cable Works Ltd		•	
General Sekiyu K.K.		•	
Hokkaido Colliery & Steamship Co. Ltd	•	•	•
Japan Steel Works Ltd	•	•	•
Mitsui Air & Sea Service Co. Ltd		•	•
Mitsui Aluminium Co. Ltd		•	
Mitsui Aluminium Co. Ltd		•	•
Mitsui & Co. Ltd	•	•	•
Mitsui Bank Ltd	•	•	•
Mitsui Coke Co. Ltd		•	•
Mitsui Concrete Industries Co. Ltd		•	
Mitsui Construction Co. Ltd	•	•	•
Mitsui Consultants Co. Ltd		•	
Mitsui Engineering & Shipbuilding Co. Ltd	•	•	•
Mitsui Harbour and Urban Construction Co. Ltd		•	
Mitsui Home Co. Ltd		•	
Mitsui Kanko Development Co. Ltd		•	•
Mitsui Knowledge Industry Co. Ltd		•	
Mitsui Leasing & Development Ltd		•	•
Mitsui Lumber Co. Ltd		•	
Mitsui Metal Processing Co. Ltd		•	
Mitsui Miike Machinery Co. Ltd		•	•
Mitsui Mining Company Ltd	•	•	
Mitsui Mining & Smelting Co. Ltd	•	•	•
Mitsui Mutual Life Insurance Co.	•	•	•
Mitsui Norin Co. Ltd		•	
Mitsui Ocean Development & Engineering Co. Ltd		•	
Mitsui Oil Exploration Co. Ltd		•	•

Company	N	G	K
Mitsui Oil Co Ltd	•	•	•
Mitsui O.S.K. Lines Ltd	•	•	•
Mitsui Petrochemical Industries Ltd		•	•
Mitsui Pharmaceuticals Inc.		•	•
Mitsui Precon Co. Ltd		•	
Mitsui Real Estate Development Co. Ltd	•	•	•
Mitsui Real Estate Sales Co. Ltd		•	•
Mitsui Seiki Kogyo Co. Ltd		•	
Mitsui Sugar Co. Ltd		•	•
Mitsui Toatsu Chemicals Inc.	•	•	•
Mitsui Trust and Banking Co. Ltd	•	•	•
Mitsui Warehouse Co. Ltd	•	•	•
Mitsui Wharf Co. Ltd		•	
Mitsukoshi Ltd	•	•	•
Nippon Flour Mills Co. Ltd	•	•	•
Nippon Univac Kaisha Ltd		•	•
Nishi Nippon Electric Wire & Cable Co. Ltd	•	•	
Oji Paper Co. Ltd	•	•	
Onoda Cement Co. Ltd	•	•	
Sanki Engineering Co. Ltd	•	•	•
Shin Nippon Air Conditioning Engineering Co. Ltd		•	
Showa Aircraft Industry Co. Ltd	•	•	
Taisho Marine and Fire Insurance Co. Ltd		•	•
Taito Co. Ltd		•	
Toray Engineering Co. Ltd		•	
Toray Industries Inc.		•	•
Toshiba Corp.		•	
Toshuku Ltd		•	•
Toyo Engineering Corp.		•	
Toyo Menka Kaisha Ltd		•	•
Toyota Motor Co. Ltd (Observer)	•	•	

(N) Second Thursday Presidents' Club; (G) Monday Club of Presidents; (K) Public Relations Directors' Club

Figure 4.1 The main companies of the Mitsui Group, linked by clubs

These interconnections give the group great power in international markets (see Figure 4.2). The commercial installations are outside Japan in high-consumption areas, while the big projects of the future are in areas of greatest ease of operations and maximum manpower and raw materials. Mitsui's history seems to us exemplary in the way its managers reacted to the American restraints. Just as impressive was the way the executives were able to create a group of companies of various sizes in various sectors of industry, interrelated in new ways that would have seemed comic in another time. But no one is laughing now, because the results are there after more than twenty years of progress on a grand scale.

Four goals have been set for Mitsui's next fifteen years:

- Securing raw material sources, and entering the big consumer markets.

- Aid to countries developing their industrial infrastructures.

- Transfer of advanced technology to countries wishing to develop sophisticated industrial complexes.

- Development of major social and educational activities.

Mitsui has become the world's second largest group after Mitsubishi – a good lesson from the former *zaibatsu*.

The Japanese banks, which had no industrial activity at all, were able to create groups from their clients, and co-ordinate them in the truest sense. Thus the Dai-Ichi Kangyo Bank (DKB), after the first oil shock, helped its clients in difficulty to get back on their feet, and had by 1978 created from scratch a family of companies that it organized in the Third Friday of the Month Club, which brought together forty-five chairmen from companies as diverse as photography, insurance, chemicals, cars, farm machinery, etc. Other groups sprang up around other banks, such as Fuyo, Sanwa, etc. So the movement has grown. Industrial companies noted the success of the *zaibatsu* and bank groups, and created groups around themselves, such as Nippon Steel, Hitachi, Nissan, Toyota, Matsushita, Ihi, Sord, etc. Of all these groups, Nippon Steel and Komatsu are the most interesting. We offer their cases in some detail.

The Nippon Steel story: how to create productivity and full employment in a recession

The Nippon Steel family today includes 666 companies, of which 60 are umbrella organizations responsible for group policy (52 in Japan, 8 abroad) and linked by contact among their managers; 127 are level 2 companies; and 479 are level 3. Equity participation breaks down as follows:

Level 1 Majority holdings 59
Level 2 Holdings between 20 per cent and 5 per cent 157
Level 3 Holdings from 0 per cent to 20 per cent 450

In addition to club meetings the presidents of the level 1 and level 2 companies meet once a year. The managers of these same companies meet twice a year, mainly to present their quality-control achievements. A 'central management group' of about thirty people, including three directors, co-ordinates the various activities that result in the good management of the Nippon Steel family. This management group reviews the year-end balance sheets of the top 187 companies, administers the detachment for various periods of nearly 1000 managers from the umbrella organization for assignments in companies of the group, and administers nearly 400 retired employees assigned to these same companies. The detachment of employees, who are not allowed to total more than a fixed number per company, amounts to career enhancement and opportunity for the men concerned, and a source of technical assistance for the companies.

In more general terms the central management group assumes the following missions:

● Engineering for new factories, notably to produce new products.

● Development of total quality-control (TQC) programmes in the companies.

	Oceania	North and Central America		South America
Peking	Guam	Montreal	Phoenix	Caracas
Tianjin	Port Moresby	Toronto	Los Angeles	Port of Spain
Dalian	Honiara	Calgary	San Francisco	La Paz
Shanghai	Perth	Vancouver	San Diego	Belem
Guangzhou	Melbourne	New York	Portland	Brasilia
	Sydney	Washington DC	Seattle	Belo Horizonte
	Brisbane	Pittsburgh	Bermuda	Rio de Janeiro
	Wellington	Cleveland	Havana	Sao Paulo
	Auckland	Detroit	Mexico City	Cascavel
	Noumea	Chicago	Monterrey	Buenos Aires
	Honolulu	Charlotte	Guatemala	Santiago
		Atlanta	San Salvador	Lima
		Memphis	Managua	Guayaquil
		Miami	Panama	Quito
		Denver		Bogota
		Houston		
		Dallas		
		Obregon		
		Calexico		

Europe and USSR		Africa and Middle East	Asia		
Helsinki	Vienna	Tripoli	Ankara	Karachi	Bangkok
Stockholm	Prague	Tunis	Beyrouth	Lahore	Hatyai
Oslo	Luxembourg	Algeria	Damas	Islamabad	Vientiane
Namur	Paris	Casablanca	Amman	New Delhi	Hong Kong
Warsaw	Bucarest	Las Palmas	Jeddah	Bombay	Djakarta
Berlin	Budapest	Abidjan	Riyadh	Goa	Kuching
Hamburg	Sofia	Lagos	Abu Dhabi	Hyderabad	Kata Kinabalu
Frankfurt	Athens	Doula	Dubai	Bangalore	Sandakan
Munich	Belgrade	Kinshasa	Ajman	Cochin	Davao
Dusseldorf	Rome	Luanda	Al-Khobar	Colombo	Bacolod
Amsterdam	Milan	Johannesburg	Damman	Madras	Manila
Rotterdam	Madrid	Dar es Salaam	Sanaa	Bhubaneswar	Kaohsiung
Brussels	Barcelona	Lusaka	Kuwait	Calcutta	Taipei
London	Valencia	Kitwe	Bagdad	Dacca	Seoul
Dublin	Lisbon	Tananarive	Teheran	Chittagong	Masan
Cork	Moscow	Nairobi	Bahrain	Rangoon	Pusan
		Addis Ababa	Doha	Kuala Lumpur	Ulsan
		Khartoum	Muscat	Singapore	Pohang
		Le Caire			
		Istanbul			

Figure 4.2   The main facilities of the Mitsui companies

- Distribution of training literature throughout the affiliates.

- Optimizing the allocation of advanced technical equipment.

- Organizing meetings and conferences (for example, on quality circles).

- Plant visits to provide diagnosis of problems, to perform audits, to advise, etc.

Several of these services have become so renowned that now Nippon Steel clients are even demanding their help. The development of Nippon Steel includes three main thrusts, all of which are complementary. The first is productivity improvement and the stimulation of the pace of progress in such areas as TQC.

An effective TQC system involves a number of activities:

- For any new company entering the group, thorough training and background information is given to all managers.

- Seminars are held at all levels on the importance of reducing costs, waste, inventories, breakdowns, and on the need to conserve energy.

- Seminars are organized on quality circles – their strategy and objectives, and methods for implementing QC techniques.

- An annual TQC congress is organized, plus a separate congress for women employees.

- Training of conference leaders who have already completed university-level business courses.

The second main thrust at Nippon Steel is diversification. More than ten years ago the company decided to undertake a serious diversification programme, even though the recession had hit the firm (less severely, however, than foreign steelmakers). Indeed the company made progress during part of the recessionary years because of its productivity gains.

The objective was to build a stronger foundation for the company and ensure its future growth. The method for achieving this goal was not to rely on its traditional products but to create new products that would be consumed worldwide tomorrow. These attitudes were not sufficient to spare Nippon Steel serious problems. It turned out that the general policy of lifetime employment (that is, full employment) caused formidable difficulties, because great strides in productivity were being made and meant large numbers of employees were no longer needed. Recession in some markets made things worse.

Nippon Steel decided therefore to expand its investment in diversification, so that the creation of new jobs in its new businesses would compensate for the loss of jobs in its traditional activities. More recently, as the average life-span has increased and the younger workers have been unable to finance the cost of retirement, the company decided to put back retirement age by five years. In 1981 the retirement age was 55, and it rose to 60 at the end of 1985 – adding another 1500 people to the already overloaded payroll.

To continue to maintain full employment the company decided a few years ago to put even more emphasis on its diversification programme. In the first years new projects were related to the steel industry. Now they are moving into a wide variety of businesses – agriculture, real estate, travel agencies, printing and others.

The third thrust is in the rotation of personnel. We have already discussed how the company manages the rotation of some 1500 employees – managers or experienced retired persons – in companies that make up the group. In the same way the excess manpower of some of the companies is also redirected towards the new activities, where the new jobs are being created. Incidentally the success of these new businesses is aided by management input, by constant progress towards total quality control, and by the interaction of the managers, who exchange ideas, technologies and strategies. Obviously a heavy training regime is required.

Today some 10 per cent of Nippon Steel turnover is made up of diversified activities. When we visited the company, our hosts summed up their presentation by saying: 'Today it is not a question of making money, but of assuring the continuation of the group in the long term; and while awaiting the results, we can say that so far diversification has been profitable for us'.

The Komatsu story: How to beat your fiercest competitor

In 1961, following the liberation of restrictions in Japan, the giant American company Caterpillar made a massive move into the Japanese market. Komatsu, operating in the same business, but on a much smaller scale, felt its survival was in danger, especially considering that Komatsu products were only about half as reliable as those of the American giant. The main challenge facing Komatsu was to raise the quality of its bulldozers to a level clearly above that of Caterpillar – and to accomplish this without delay. Simultaneously Komatsu introduced a new quality-control system for all products in the company. Today the Komatsu group has accomplished its mission; it has won the battle. The group now includes several hundred companies – various suppliers, subsidiaries, distributors (domestic and foreign) and other affiliates.

The parent company has a capital of only $174 million, and a payroll of 17 000. But 70 per cent of its components come from outside suppliers. The distributors are responsible for pre-sale activities and after-sales service. Annual sales were $835 million in 1983, and exports account for 64 per cent of sales. Another sign of the group's good health is that in 1983 Komatsu distributed to each employee the equivalent of $5\frac{1}{2}$ months' salary as a year-end bonus for 1982 performance.

How did Komatsu do it? One of the keys to its success is that, beginning in 1961 and continuing to this day, Komatsu has implemented a series of action plans: first for survival, then for development, and continuously for the creation of a family of companies – those upstream (raw materials, basic components) and those downstream (end-users) whether small, medium or large. The aim has been to optimize the service–quality–price ratio of the company's products by

stimulating constant progress in each company at all levels
– from conception and development through delivery to
customers.

Here is the chronology of the company's key action plans:

In 1961 the first plan to improve service and reliability
of its basic product, the bulldozer, is launched.
In 1962 the same plan is applied to all other products
in the company.
In 1965 the president launches a cost-reduction programme,
and extends the original 1961 plan to foreign operations.
Since 1969, various other plans have been launched, some
with specific objectives, or challenges to meet, as in a series
of battles that must be won in order to win the war.
In 1976 the Komatsu Prize to encourage better quality
throughout the group is created.

Here are some of the most original features of the Komatsu
plans.

1   The objectives of Total Quality Control (TQC)

The success of TQC was cited when the company won the
Deming Prize in 1965, and is one of the criteria of the
Komatsu Prize. Winning the internal prize is a long and
laborious process. When the winner is chosen, its personnel
will have completed elaborate training and the company itself
submitted to a variety of severe measurements and evaluations of its progress.

2   Komatsu training

Komatsu has created several large training centres. As an
example, Table 4.1 shows training plans for quality circles
techniques.

3   Evaluation system for the Komatsu Prize

Results of the company are periodically examined. Here is
a summary of the items evaluated for the prize (the points
are weighted):

Table 4.1
Quality Circles training

Types of training	Categories	Hours
Obligatory	Directors	10
	Department heads	38
	Technicians	32
	Administrators	24
	Supervisors	24
	Workers	24
	New employees	8
For specialists	Basic Course A	192
	Basic Course B	114
	Reliability	?
	Experimentation	40
	Various other methods	?

(a) Management index (80 points)

● Sales to profit ratio (20)

● Break-even ratio (20)

● Added value per person ratio (20)

● Sales and balance sheet (20)

(b) Quality control (200 points)

● Returns (35)

● Waste during production (20)

● Number of controls not applied (20)

● Distribution ratio (30)

● Variance between forecast and results   (70)

● Variance between estimates and actual energy savings

● Number of theses in QCs

● Number of QCs and percentage of personnel participating

- One additional ratio determined by the company (25)

(c) Organization and functioning of the company (320 points)

- Application of policy (37 points)
- Quality assurance (52)
- Distribution (25)
- Cost control (36)
- Training for and functioning of quality circles (15)
- Progress in raising qualifications and improving the technique of achieving unity (15)
- Level of industrial production (140)

The evaluations are made throughout the year, and results are discussed in groups made up of representatives of several companies. The name of the company under discussion is not revealed to the group. Any direct criticism is offered in private by men from the headquarters evaluation team. The evaluation chart is designed to fit each type of 'family' member: subsidiary, sub-contractor, distributor, both domestic and foreign.

4 Technical assistance from headquarters to group companies

This service covers a broad area, including training, headquarters culture, and technical and advisory services in such areas as industrial costs, quality assurance, energy savings, etc.

5 Linkage of companies, and the selling of the Komatsu culture

Weaving the companies together and implanting a common culture happens at the top in the club system, and elsewhere in all kinds of in-company associations, conferences and seminars.

6   Central structure of group management

The vice-president has under him the Total Quality Control High Committee as well as thirty-five departments, but the men heading them are so thoroughly imbued with company policy and horizontal co-operation that it is rarely necessary for the vice-president to have to arbitrate in disputes.

These thirty-five departments can be grouped in four main categories:

- Departments monitoring company functions such as corporate planning, human resources, training, quality assurance (19).

- Departments responsible for industrial development of factories (6).

- Departments responsible for sales and after-sales service, domestic and international (7).

- Departments responsible for research (3).

5 The why and how of inter-company collaboration

It is one thing to describe how three companies have grown up in similar ways, but is quite another to interpret this phenomenon, and it is still riskier to try to draw conclusions that will provide insight into the world of industrial Japan. So what follows will be an attempt to look at the common strengths of the companies, and at some of the lessons that might be more or less transferable to other companies. We make no claim to have been exhaustive in our description, nor have we tried to imagine what we did not actually see.

The big groups have a much better chance than smaller individual companies to realize the full potential of their member firms. Together the goals of each company can be achieved, whereas on its own each company might achieve only part of its objective or miss it altogether.

The potential of a company can be expressed in various ways. Japanese companies, and more and more of the high-performance European firms, define their potential in these four ways:

1 *The human element.* The development of human potential, the real wealth of the group. After all, what is a company but a group of people, a 'family' united

to live an adventure, which is to bring to other people products or services designed to fit their needs.

2 *Production.* The output of products or services that meet optimum standards of utility, quality and price.

3 *The creation of wealth.* The first two points require money to be meaningful. Money must be paid to the workers, to shareholders, to machine suppliers to keep equipment up to date, and in taxes. This is the third potential of the company, to which we have given the name 'creation of wealth', because more is generated than is strictly required for the operation of the company and the payment of its workers.

4 *Good citizenship.* The company makes up one of the vital elements of the nation, essential for society's survival. Taxes must be paid of course, but in addition the company creates 'citizen earners' who are fulfilled, developed, happy to distribute quality products that improve the socio-economic and industrial image of the country, create the products of tomorrow that will reduce the need for imports, and finally maintain and develop employment.

Now let us consider the virtues of the group:

• The social and professional blossoming of people is made easier by the career openings in a large group than in a small group.

• The methods available to a large group are infinitely more diverse than in an isolated company (even a big one) for the production of high-quality goods, designed for the market, produced at a competitive price, using the synergy of employees' ideas and techniques.

We concluded that in Japan the creation of wealth arose from the very fabric of society, in that the most developed and dynamic companies provided help for the smaller members of the family to move along the path of progress, much as a locomotive pulls a goods train loaded with products that are good for all.

The Japanese do not spend time and money building up these groups just for the fun of it. They do it out of a sense of duty and spirit of excellence towards each other (for example, the head of a family towards others), and also because it pays. In the West this kind of direct commitment to the company is rare. Companies where it is done best advance rapidly, but the others limp along behind or end up being rescued with state funds.

The big Japanese companies, as is well known, instituted the concept of lifetime employment. No company in isolation could sustain such a policy for long, especially in a climate of recession or during a push for greater productivity, where workforces tend to shrink most radically in the consumer-products businesses. But in a large Japanese company that stimulates enthusiasm and a sense of progress, as opposed to a defensive posture, full employment in the group can be maintained, even developed, by moving employees efficiently from shrinking businesses to expanding ones. Clearly it is better for these large 'locomotive' companies to spend money, a lot of money, on diversification, retraining and housing allowances than on unemployment benefit to workers who have become useless, bitter, and thrown out into the street to live at the expense of the state.

With this group system and the full-employment scheme, the Japanese are winning on all fronts, including morale. One of the keys to their success has been that these companies took their own initiative in the quest for security of employment, without relying on law or regulation. This independence gives them the maximum flexibility on a case by case basis.

Monitoring the environment

Large groups of companies (especially Japanese groups), made up of small, medium and large firms, are infinitely better placed to forecast tomorrow's market than are smaller companies in isolation. We are convinced that the large intelligence networks provide an incomparable wealth of information of all kinds. These large groups – Mitsubishi, Mitsui,

Sumitomo, DKB or Nippon Steel – are thus able to plan and develop their long-term futures ten to fifteen years ahead in tune with the evolution of markets and national economies, relying on their linkages through meetings, and exchange and synthesis of information. At their summit meetings the chairmen and presidents discuss the long-term potential of their companies as well as their ethical principles. The directors draw up the best strategies for the next three to five years, profiting to the maximum from all the synergy the group can provide. Each company, well placed to adapt to new circumstances and to take advantage of opportunities, implements the tactical action plan with the best chance of success, confident that it fits in with the group's future plans.

Management development

It is quite surprising to see what remarkable managers Japan is able to produce. Yet they have no material resources (except people) and few management schools or business schools comparable to those in the United States and Europe.

In our research, we were curious to learn how they train their managers. We found the answer, but it is not really exportable. We could never adopt their ways without completely changing our present system. Here is the Japanese way.

The first years of a future manager's career are spent at the bottom of the ladder in several functions. The object is to see that managers know the people in the company and their jobs very well.

The following years are spent moving from job to job at a responsible level in staff and line positions in various locations. The group plays an important role in this process, finding places for these men in a variety of jobs, domestic and foreign.

Still farther along the career path the best of the young managers are given the opportunity for real training – in the interlinking meetings. This is where top managers experiment with decentralization, where they discover the true nature of a given problem, all of which gives them a totally different view from that of the specialist.

Lastly, throughout their careers, Japanese managers are given strong doses of training, and they embark on equally enriching study and research missions.

The global dimension

A global dimension is of course not an end in itself. Inventors of new products, and founders of new companies to produce them, will always have a reasonable future, at least in countries where their activities are welcome. Statistics show that most new products come out of small and medium-sized companies. But as soon as the business grows, and the company decides to go after larger markets, it enters the competitive international world, where there are special problems of growth and distribution.

At the early stage of the new product the group can be a big help to the small company. But at the international stage the big company becomes even more useful – even indispensable. It is clear that the group system in Japan is organized to foster the development of its companies, which in turn strengthens and enlarges the group. We found it quite untrue that the small companies in Japan suffer at the hands of large firms. While it is true that material rewards and conditions are uneven in the group, the lead companies work for the development of the smaller ones (interlinking meetings, push for progress, training courses, sharing of strategic information, etc.) to help them grow and to allow them to benefit from the size and scope of the group (in financing, technical assistance, image, distribution, international commercial outlets, etc.).

The nature of inter-company collaboration

In a word it is the diversity of these company groups that best characterizes them. Historically there are three types: the former *zaibatsu,* the bank-led groups and the groups led by large industrial companies. All encompass small, medium and large companies. All cover multiple sectors and many different products.

The groups seem to have two main guiding principles:

- Diversification, with the dual objective of creating new products or new technologies, and creating new jobs to compensate for the productivity gains through technological progress in other member companies.

- Optimization of products, in terms of service, cost and quality, which has as its aim a 'coherence of progress' all the way along the chain of companies concerned with a given product, from the source of raw materials through to end-user. Because Japanese companies are decentralized, they rarely produce anything from start to finish within the boundaries of a single company.

The ties linking companies in the group bring together the men at the top. The interweaving is dual – horizontal among those of the most important companies, and vertical in cascades down to the smaller ones (Figure 5.1).

These bonds among men are extended and diversified downwards through the directorships, and are reinforced by periodic meetings. At these meetings there is no single boss who decides: there is a concerted effort to compromise, and mutual enrichment as the decision moves towards a consensus, a common orientation. The bonds are further strengthened by an extraordinary network of meetings of large groups of managers and other employees – a schedule of conferences – held periodically, bringing together all members of the enterprises at various levels and intervals.

There are other kinds of ties that we have not had the space to examine: links such as the financing, functional collaboration and development of members; the client–supplier role of 'family' members; and the sharing of distribution channels and representation services. We formed our impressions of the spirit of these groups through conversations with ranking Japanese business executives, presidents, heads of 'family' companies, or corporate managers within

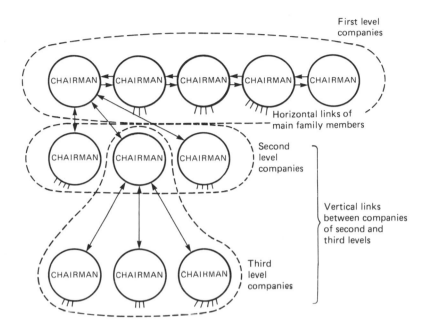

Figure 5.1   The interlinkages of chairmen in groups of companies

the group system. Without exception they gave priority to
the morale of all employees and ways to keep it high. They
all seemed attached to the notion of sharing in technological,
technical and economic progress, conveying this notion to
their associated companies in the most pragmatic and effective
way possible. They all seemed to believe that true progress
is measurable, and they showed us their measurement. It
seemed to us that Japanese managers, working in such an
environment and backed up with a lot of common sense,
could not help but succeed.

How the groups work

The groups of companies function in complex ways, some
of which we have described above. To avoid repetition we
will only point out a few unique elements.

Financial participation may or may not exist, and if it does, it is usually a small share of capital. The links are among the chairmen, but sometimes may include presidents or functional vice-presidents.

The smooth functioning of the group is a result of the system of interlinkages co-ordinated through the central office at corporate headquarters, and the barriers separating the central finance functions are not rigid obstacles – far from it. The units dedicated to the development of the group have a certain number of missions to fulfil:

- Co-ordination and administration of the linking meetings (conferences, secretariat, summaries of proceedings, distribution of information).

- Organization and co-ordination of other congresses.

- Research and development in new companies in the 'family' ('development' is defined to include industrial engineering and distribution) that bring in new products and new technologies.

- Identifying and developing the managers of the future, monitoring their progress, matching up their career paths with more senior managers and directors, organizing training programmes for them (Figure 5.2).

- Organizing the exchange of manpower in concert with diversification efforts and cutbacks in jobs in the older companies.

- Building the group's image and that of all companies in the family.

- Conception, organization and distribution throughout the group companies of progress reports (technological and others), especially in the area of training. A standard policy of revenues and borrowings, of advanced information technology, and of course the system of Total Quality Control (Table 5.1).

In all the Japanese groups we visited, TQC systems were the basic programme to be introduced, 'like it or not'. For

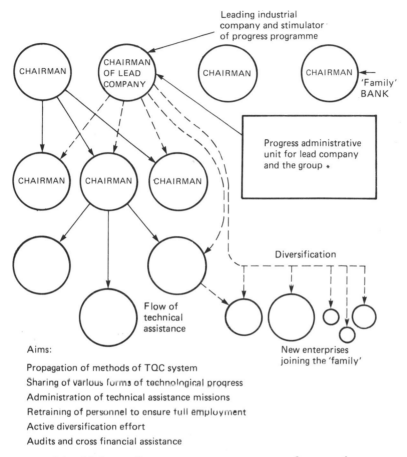

Figure 5.2   **Linkages for progress among groups of companies**

a company to obtain optimal performance in terms of cost and service to customers, TQC is seen as the path to customer satisfaction and victory over competitors. It is founded on the belief that one can always do better tomorrow than today. Thus we were often told that TQC is a responsibility of corporate management.

The TQC programme is in fact a package of complementary and synergistic actions. Among them are:

● Actions to motivate employees. For good results, the

Table 5.1
Total Quality-Control system: table of complementary actions

Actions to promote	Observations
1 Battery of statistical methods to monitor product quality	Careful adaptation required at each level
2 Reduction of costs (e.g. energy conservation)	Specific targets must be set, no compromising
3 Annual campaign to combat the phantom enterprise (zero defect, downtime, low inventories, paper, accidents, delays, etc.)	Without fail, each year, with one or two concrete objectives
4 Structure for explanations, and technical assistance. Committees, conferences, advisory groups, etc. Facilitators for QCs	These mechanisms are graduated throughout the company
5 Motivation of employees, quality circles company-wide, guidance circles, training, information groups, committees, conferences	No. 1 requirement for TQCs, full participation of employees
6 Careful measurement of progress in points 1–5	With the same precision, measure improvement in product quality (1), quality of life (5) and performance (2, 3, 4)

Encouragement of TQC system centralized at the highest level of the company and the group. Corporate headquarters organize the common core activities and audits. Decentralization can be allowed as the system begins to take root.

capacity for innovation and intelligence of everyone in the company must be mobilized. The quality-circle concept is central, and must be applied company-wide, with all that implies: special training, facilitators, and conferences inside and outside the company.

● Actions for measuring progress. Points 1 to 5 in Table 5.1 are of course measurable in detail – waste in the production process, customer rejects, the number of problems examined in quality circles, the number of meetings and their object.

● The co-ordination of points 1–6 in Table 5.1 is generally decentralized. Of course headquarters personnel perform diagnostic work, periodic checks and audits. They also conceive and distribute certain training under the 'common core' programme, and they train the facilitators for the quality circles.

Obviously the TQC system is not an abstract concept, a specialized statistical method or a random collection of hit-and-run measures. It is instead a vast concerted movement on many fronts – social, technological, economic – requiring mobilization of all companies in the group. All this must be guided by a carefully planned strategy, uniting a variety of competences under the aegis of head office administrators and top management of each company, with the active support of group top management – the chairman, president and vice-presidents.

6 Towards a new style of management

Managers of Type 3 companies know how to spot the obstacles in their path, and they know how to take advantage of them – to choose the battles they have a chance of winning. Two examples will suffice:

- To face head on the contradiction between productivity and full employment means reducing the workforce, fighting defensive battles, and seeing the company's image deteriorate as 'the company that lays off workers'. Turning this situation to the company's advantage means guaranteeing employment and adopting a policy of making the best use of employees throughout their careers. This implies large-scale training programmes, and a programme for creative diversification to find new products and new jobs.

- Facing competitive challenges means seeking ways of saving money, reducing payroll and paying heavy social security charges. A good TQC system is needed to reverse these constraints and turn them around to profit the company. The constraints come in many forms. The very nature of working life must be changed to respond to the expectations of today's generation, which in itself is an unavoidable sociological constraint. TQC must be implemented throughout the company in all activities. Well planned strategies can ensure the spread of automated office concepts and decentralized computer networks, for it is a kind of constraint on the enterprise that information must be better processed and better understood to ensure faster response to customers' needs.

Managing these constraints is best done in three phases: identification of the problem as insurmountable if tackled head on; manoeuvring around it in search of a new angle of attack from which the battle *can* be won; and devoting sufficient real resources to wage the battle successfully. This process is not an intellectual game. It leads to powerful long-term strategic action.

Qualitative management

In the old-style company, management concentrates mainly on products and money. This is the quantitative approach: overseeing production, sales and market share on the one hand, and the balance sheet and profitability on the other.

The other way is better suited to our times. Priority goes to achieving progress of all kinds in company organization, and to improve the quality of products and working life in the company – since quality of life helps determine how dynamic, inventive and motivated employees will be; quality of technology is one of the keys of productivity; and the combination of quality people with quality resources creates the best conditions for quality results.

The key to qualitative management is commitment at the top level. From the managing director's office, or just below, production quality must be pursued through a wide range of measures: minimizing waste and delays, turning over inventory, etc. The quality of working life can be measured, for example, by increasing the number of quality circles and by tracking the type and number of problems they tackle. Qualitative management requires a new approach to problems most companies have not mastered, and measurable only by new methods. The chairman of one large company told us: 'I monitor throughout the company how many problems are resolved at the level of small groups each year. If this number is growing, I can relax. It will mean that our market share will be growing'.

Managing multiple uncertainty

One Japanese chairman told us, only half in jest: 'You French are lucky to be able to read the crystal ball. You can make medium-term forecasts. But we don't know what our future holds'. But he added, not in jest: 'Long term, ten to fifteen years, we know better than you what we want to be doing'. Indeed uncertainty is best regarded as a medium-term inconvenience, not a long-term problem. This explains why the most successful companies use the 'four-speed' management technique, the scenario, and, most important of all, an attitude of permanent flexibility. These elements help a company seize the opportunities that lead to achieving that long-term objective.

Another aspect of managing uncertainty is the flood of data to take into account. Traditional managers select what they believe to be the most important facts, and decide on their own what risks to take. But managers of Type 3 companies are often able to enrich their understanding of a situation by analysing the data in groups. Members of the group can perhaps add to the information and contribute new points of view. The action that results is thus a kind of majority decision, a consensus. Obviously actions decided upon in this way are very different from those taken in executive isolation.

A third aspect of the management of uncertainty is the need to deal effectively with problems of policy, strategy and resources. Top managers of the big, high-performance companies made it clear to us that they saw their first obligations as the definition of the firm's objectives, general direction in socio-economic and technology terms, as well as its fundamental and permanent values.

Top management should draw up scenarios and the corresponding strategic plans, and apply themselves to finding the necessary resources to carry out the plans. Middle management organizes and carries out the tactical operations, seizing opportunities as they come along.

A fourth element of managing the complexities of uncertainty is 'highest-level control' of the various activities for achieving a new synergy. A note of explanation: we in the West have traditionally chopped up our companies into several separate and distinct functions (marketing, research and development, production, sales, distribution, personnel, administration, etc.), appointing a director to head each function. All the activities of the company are covered by these functions, and the director co-ordinates, arbitrates and makes the decisions. Among the activities covered are many sub-categories, such as training, quality control, energy conservation and others.

Managers are usually comfortable with the straightforward logic of this system, but orchestrating all the sub-categories can cause a certain unease. This is an area of uncertainty for managers of traditional companies in Europe, and the unease takes on greater proportions if the 'orchestration' is directed from the upper reaches of the management structure. But in Type 3 companies that is not the way it works. Functions are grouped differently, for example:

- Exploitation, which consists essentially of producing and selling products that meet customers' needs.

- Progress, which combines the permanent monitoring of the environment and training for the progress of the people.

Management of the second function is as important as management of the first. For example, running a Total Quality Control system comes under the second part, and ranks at the very top of the company structure.

Managing collaboration

The acceptance of the concept of collaboration among all employees is probably the most original characteristic of 'new

management'. It comes from the fact that companies today
need ideas from all sources in the firm – from cleaning staff
to chairman. The mechanisms for achieving this are available
and well tested: quality circles at the shop floor level, guidance
circles for middle management, and clubs for the chairmen,
presidents and directors.

To this interlocking system are added conferences and
seminars at various levels, where companies who have made
progress share their experience with others. Such widespread
collaboration has many positive effects:

- At all levels it mobilizes intellectual capability and
  ideas.

- It motivates the innovator, and gives him or her satisfaction.

- It facilitates the creation of hybrid technologies.

- It is the key to true decentralization, the kind that
  affects everyone, down to the shop floor, where workers
  respond to the humanization by showing more initiative. Viewed from the top the same decentralization
  leads to more sub-contractors and subsidiaries, thus
  more posts of managerial responsibility.

Collaboration means dialogue. It implies a managerial attitude of openness to others, including subordinates, and the
humility to believe that good ideas can come from others.
In addition it implies that the progression towards action
is best achieved by a compromise of several views, preferably
with the agreement of the highest-level contributor.

The management task

It is only a slight exaggeration to say that in our tradition
the manager is there to defend his turf and the position to
which he has been appointed. The manager has been chosen
because he is the best, and he feels compelled to reinforce
his image by frequent manifestations of authority. We are
in a situation where the manager has rights over his domain.

But a Type 3 company manager must adopt a very different attitude. His job is to develop the fullest potential of his subordinates so that the group as a whole can move more effectively towards a common objective. He has a tendency to step back and allow another in the group to draw him out. His approach is one of a seminar leader rather than an authoritarian. We are now in a situation where a manager has a duty towards others to motivate and weld them into a team strong enough to win the battle.

The two profiles of manager, old and new, fit into two kinds of structure:

- The traditional pyramid, made up of divisions, departments and services, and well-defined territory. Much time and effort is devoted to defending it.

- The multifaceted, flexible structure whose shape evolves as objectives are set and then attained or surpassed.

The traditional manager gives orders, and has relatively little contact with the lower echelon. The Type 3 manager spends much of his time in contact with employees at all levels – an activity otherwise known as MBWA, or management by wandering around.

Management development

We noted in Chapter 2 that Japanese managers are moulded by the enterprise, in a series of career moves across functions, and by collaborating and interlinking mechanisms. There are two other important considerations:

- Good managers are developed over the long term. Basing the success of the enterprise on a single talented individual can sometimes be sufficient, but cannot be the general rule.

- Good managers are developed by forcing men and

women to deal with many different situations in a variety of functions.

We need a great many good managers to ensure our future. It would be wise to let the best companies be our guide. They prepare their managers step by step, planning for them a round of geographical and professional assignments, continuously evaluating their performance and granting them 'credit' for progress only insofar as they improve the performance of their group.

The middle manager

All this attention to top-management responsibility should not reduce the importance of middle management, which ties together the senior levels and the shop floor. The Type 3 make demands not only on high-level management but on middle managers, who also are very different from their traditional brethren.

In the companies, there is no 'middle management malaise' because the competitive battles are well defined, and the managers are very busy trying to win them. How? In fulfilling five distinct but complementary missions (Figure 6.1):

1   *Participation in formulating the mission.* The middle managers contribute their suggestions, and play their part in developing short-term and medium-term action plans.

2   *Explanation of the mission.* The middle managers describe the mission to their subordinates, discussing the objectives, their strong points, their difficulties. They answer questions, and collect opinions and suggestions for improving the mission or facilitating its implementation.

3   *Organization of the performance-improvement efforts, the campaigns for progress.* The managers plan and carry out the tactical operations, seizing opportunities and optimizing the use of resources. This part is particu-

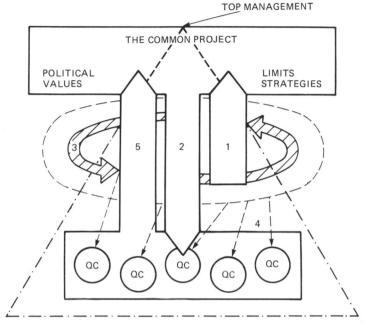

Figure 6.1 Middle management's role

larly concerned with the 'guidance circles' of the middle management level.

4 *Leading shop-floor workers and other subordinates.* The managers mobilize the intelligence, the new ideas of their subordinates and apply them in operational plans. To this end they create quality circles, and oversee the functioning of technical assistance and training and orientation efforts.

5 *TQC analysis, worker participation, presentations.* The managers take into account all the solutions that emerge from the quality circles. Of course Total Quality Control would mean nothing without the participative element – the gradual collection of dozens or hundreds of small improvements that add up to a great result.

But even this is not enough. To show the workers that their contributions are important, managers must systematically organize presentations from the quality circles to their superiors, and show off the best ideas to conferences or seminars inside and outside the company.

Six key words sum up the attitudes middle managers should adopt: listening, dialogue, humility, training, leadership, professionalism.

Agenda for action: ten ways to get started

There is no single way to move a company from traditional management into the realm of the Type 3 enterprise. Every company is a special case; every company has its own complex personality, with obvious differences in managerial style, product specialities, production methods, organizational structure, strengths and weaknesses, traditions or corporate culture. A company is the sum of these complexities, and creating change calls for a great deal of perseverance and care. This is why we always counsel against trying to make too many changes at the same time. As in organ transplants, a rejection syndrome can quickly sabotage the most vigorous efforts.

Chances of success are best when changes:

- are actively endorsed by top management,

- fill a real need in the company and respond to employee's expectations,

- are adopted enthusiastically by middle management,

- are matched by specially earmarked financial resources.

The entire effort is given a boost of credibility if the first phase of change is a success. Employees are happy to take on tasks of analysis or innovation different from their daily routine. So an initial success can open the door to others of greater importance. The launch must be underpinned by a sound 'diagnosis', and fit into a medium-term plan.

1 *Introduction,* in which changes are superficial and minor in appearance, and focus on the initial stage. The object is to break away from the status quo, to experiment without taking big risks, and to make employees understand that future changes might be coming.
2 *The pilot projects,* where change is made in specific operations in a more basic way, and with more muscle applied. These changes are selected as a result of experience gained from phase 1.
3 *Company-wide implementation* then follows from the first two phases, and obstacles can be better foreseen. The change can be applied to all activities, driven by the financial and other resources released for the programme.

The three phases may require as long as two to five years, depending on the size of the company and the type of changes being implemented. Obviously a strong and steady commitment from top management will be the key to making the effort successful.

We have identified ten 'entry points' for starting the Type 3 company process. All of them provide a 'leverage effect' that helps to promote further change. For the sake of clarity we shall look at each one separately, but in practice companies will be found implementing them in almost any combination – often producing useful synergy in the process.

1 Dialogue and 'decentralized credits'

One of the most interesting examples of internal dialogue can be found in the French company Lesieur. More than ten years ago, Lesieur's top management initiated a series of meetings in all departments and services, led by the senior supervisor, to encourage employees to speak their minds and discuss problems among themselves. The leader's main role is to listen (if he talks too much, there is no point holding the meeting). He must also show some humility (if he believes no subordinate is capable of contributing a good idea, there is also no point holding the meeting). The aim of the meetings is to select the best suggestions and begin the process of implementing them. This kind of dialogue can be generated at any level with any combination of specialities. What is essential is that the meetings be held in the work area, because it is at this level that the little problems of daily working life are as important. They must be solved by those who know them best.

To finance the solution Lesieur grants a credit of 500 francs (about £50) per year per person. Middle management has no veto over the decisions, but does have a duty to organize the selection of the best solutions, and to see that they are rapidly implemented. Lesieur calls this fund a 'decentralized credit', and includes it in the annual budget on a special line for improvement of working conditions. The first objective is to foster the elimination of all the little problems of daily working life that seem petty viewed separately but in sum add up to important problems. The second objective is to remove the obstacles that block a trusting and harmonious relationship from top management to middle management to the workers' level. If the workers are expected to support the grand vision of progress spelled out by top management, the first step in gaining credibility should be to listen to the suggestions from below to improve daily working conditions. Experience shows that the improvements are always concentrated in areas such as productivity, waste and the physical working conditions. Dialogue and 'decentralized credits' are among the best methods of achieving a climate that in turn allows for other, more fundamental changes, such as the benefits of quality circles.

2 Quality circles

Quality circles (QCs) are one of the most effective means of bringing about basic change without seeming to do so. Inaugurating the first quality circles is easily done in any company where there is an area obviously ripe for improvement. The reaction from workers is always very positive, because they are waiting for an opportunity to offer their ideas – and they have plenty at hand – to apply to their working environment.

QCs can produce a cascade of change as they become more common throughout the company, and eventually affect the majority of employees. Here are some of the possibilities presented by QCs:

- Dealing with the immediate, short-term problems, working conditions, product quality, security, etc.

- Perfecting the structure and organization of the QCs themselves, and development of new skills for QC members by the new kinds of tasks handed down from middle management to the circles.

- Development of new qualifications for QC members, and opening of new career possibilities for them.

- Better mastery of the production process, improvement in product quality, productivity and quality assurance, reduction of costs.

- Significant improvement in financial performance, once the number of employees taking part exceeds 50 per cent.

- Change in the structure of communications and management (a broad trend towards decentralization) and new style from senior management, which evolves from authority symbol to facilitator.

The QCs are clearly the best lever to 'de-Taylorize' a company at the worker level, to reconcile man and his work, and to establish communication among different parts of the structure. But beyond this the QCs are one of the key factors in the Total Quality Control system described in earlier chapters. It is the TQC systems that allow self-policing of quality standards, thereby providing the company the best form of quality assurance.

We indicated above that the launching of QCs can be brought about gradually from above. But is this the best route? The answer is 'no' if top management is not willing to take the entire programme in hand; but the answer is 'yes' if the senior management team assumes the responsibility for guiding the system, perseveres with its implementation, and makes frequent visible gestures of support and encouragement by participating in the presentations and conferences and seminars relating to the QC effort.

There is no doubt that the best QC-development strategy is that led by a top management team convinced that the company must be de-Taylorized – that the state of mind and methods of management must be changed. Transformations can be gradually and progressively implemented from above, by initiatives such as conditioning employees for change, disseminating information and training, and putting the financial and other material resources in place. These resources include trainers, facilitators, technical assistance, committees, systems for measuring progress, etc. All this must be worked into a plan for quality, or, better yet, integrated into a series of actions leading towards a Total Quality Control system.

The first three mechanisms may seem separate and distinct; actually they are related.

3 Hunting down the 'phantom company'

The 'phantom company' is made up of all the 'added value' effort that does not show up in the finished product – but must be added to the cost. Sometimes this represents a big proportion of the selling price. Some of the elements in the 'phantom' costs, you will recall, are production rejects and needlessly high inventories. These concepts are now being popularized in some companies by such programmes as the 'Zero Olympics', in which teams strive for zero waste, zero inventories, zero delay, zero defect, zero breakdown, zero paper, zero accident, etc.

In the typical Taylorite enterprise the organization of production and quality control allows for a certain level of quality of finished product, and experience establishes standards that become the target to maintain. Falling below the standard then triggers corrective action. But in Type 3 companies there is no fixed 'acceptable standard'. Workers are constantly striving to improve the system, or, if necessary, they are changing the system. Not only have we discovered that great progress is possible, but we have invented new means of measurement, new kinds of management. We now know that the Taylor-based system has suppressed tremendous potential, on a scale we never would have suspected. The cost of poor-quality production and the potential for improvement in overcoming the 'phantom' can amount to 10 to 20 per cent of turnover, sometimes more.

The most effective mode of attack on the phantom enterprise or the phantom factory is the Total Quality Control system discussed in earlier chapters. A TQC system properly implemented, with its interacting and complementary elements – supported from above by training, committee meetings, mechanisms for assistance – can produce results in four fields:

- Motivation through participation in the programme, and a greater sense of satisfaction.

- Improvement in product quality.

- A rise in productivity.

- Improvement in bottom-line performance.

It follows then that a fair distribution of the additional profit should be arranged among the four normal channels for profits: taxes, investment, repayment of loans, and the employees. For the employees a profit-sharing scheme can be combined with additional compensation on the basis of improvements realized in the 'phantom company' exercise or the 'Zero Olympics' effort. This can be one of the most effective ways of shaking off the old Taylor tradition and moving into the age of the Type 3 company.

4   Interlinking company presidents

Collaborating with other companies is perhaps the newest idea for Western industrialists – but it is also one with great promise and potential. In previous chapters we described the interlinking of company presidents through weekly and monthly clubs, and how these contacts created 'families' that united several thousand companies. We have seen how these links allow companies to achieve objectives that no company on its own could hope to reach. In Europe managers meet colleagues at a variety of associations and conferences, but they in effect leave their specific company problems at the door. These organizations discuss business, but almost never the performance or management of a company – a basic difference between us and the Japanese. We keep company business to ourselves, but the Japanese presidents talk about 'family' members' industrial and commercial direction, they exchange information, they discuss joint ventures or other forms of collaboration. They compare notes on TQC systems, computerization, compensation. They also bring in outside personalities and they make business proposals to the guests, with all the weight of the 'family' behind them.

Europeans would be wise to take a tip from the Japanese, and together move towards the changes that must be made for their own good. This need is what they have in common even though they may be in different industries and from companies of different sizes.

5   Training the middle management cadre

All Type 3 companies distribute a manual or book of policy that helps establish a common culture for the entire firm. Often every employee is taught the culture – first of all, top management. What sets the Type 3 company apart is the degree of decentralization and autonomy in each unit. This improves 'response time' to each event at the working level, and helps guarantee consistency, thanks to the deep penetration of policy and strategy throughout the company.

When a tradition-bound company decides to evolve into a Type 3 company, the complexity of the mission must not be underestimated, as we warned earlier. When the Type 3 changes are in place, the company's thirst for growth, diversification and conquest can become magnified tenfold.

This is where the middle management cadre should be brought in.

The mission encompasses the values and limitations of the enterprise, job by job, product by product. It also takes into account all possible scenarios, medium-term plans and preparations for tactical action (see Chapter 1). The employees must be made to understand and share the general objectives, to be aware of the socio-economic environment, to realize there are obstacles to be overcome and the strategies to do so, on such different levels as the human, the financial, the industrial and the sales side.

A training programme for achieving these objectives might contain:

● Training modules for all employees, regardless of rank. This is the common core of the programme.

● Special modules for different parts of the company, keyed to the peculiarities of the department.

● General corporate culture modules normally presented by outside consultants, as opposed to internal modules that must be developed by insiders.

● Modules on the behaviour of the personnel.

These four modules can be presented in several ways: at discussion meetings, internal case studies, at conferences off the premises, and during preparations for full-scale action plans that are based on the units' strategy. In summary, the modules are intended to help middle management to move the company towards achieving a Type 3 system, and to assume its new role in the new order.

6   Guidance circles and the encouragement of strategic reflection

All recent studies of middle management speak of the widening gap between the managers' expectations and reality. When managers at the French company Cofremca were surveyed, the results showed that they wanted more autonomy and personal growth, and more contact with others. They also demonstrated an unexpected taste for a fight and for risk. Yet most companies seem dull, ordinary, grey, over-centralized, locked into organization charts and rigid procedures. In other words, many companies seem designed for men and women reduced to their simplest technical dimension.

Guidance circles help unblock this kind of company. Just as quality circles broaden the horizons of shop-floor workers, sales teams and others, guidance circles offer the various levels of middle management an opportunity to help work out the strategic plans for the unit to which they are assigned.

A wide range of improvements can be made rapidly, once the groups of five to ten persons at each level (division, department, plant, service) are established and the work begins on such items as analysis of missions and examination of the units' potential. For example, the guidance circle of one service centre in a company receives its mission from a superior level, perhaps departmental administration. The guidance circle can make full use of its freedom of action to accomplish the mission. Indeed the circle can set its own targets higher than those imposed from above. It is in these meetings that each member of the circle develops his or her abilities to think strategically. The circle helps prepare its members for promotion, where more and more strategic skills will be required. In traditionally managed companies much time and effort is lost on newly promoted executives who have not been prepared for their new level of work.

The guidance circles also have other important functions:

- A true dissemination from top to bottom of the company's policies, objectives and missions.

- Enrichment of the company's strategies, top to bottom, as each level makes an effort to use its freedom to achieve more and better than the targets.

- Determination of priorities to propose to the quality circles.

7   The shared mission

The motives behind senior management's decision to explain and elaborate on a company's mission are bound to differ. No two companies go about the communication process the same way. One company may spell out the long-term targets it wishes to achieve, another may want to speak only in inspirational terms of the task to be achieved, yet another may want to try to foster a consensus on the stimulation of new ideas. Whatever the differences in objectives, however, the most important thing is not the project itself but the methods employed to bring together the men and women of the company.

Whatever the company, all projects eventually touch on these three themes and their sub-themes:

FRAMEWORK
   Goal
   Objective
   Identity
   Vocation
   Grand design
   Destiny
   Mission
   Ambition
COHESIVENESS
   Values
   Code of conduct
   Culture
   Invariables
   Morale
   Restrictions
ACTION
   Objectives for progress
   Programmes
   Direction of policy

Employees might participate in different ways in the development of the three themes, but in successful companies these programmes all have one thing in common: their top managements do not simply pronounce their views, then go on to other things. Top management commits itself to the programme and remains committed, encouraging dialogue and debate, helping in the process to build a new sense of solidarity among all employees.

8 A business intelligence system

Any decision to open the company's eyes on the outside world must necessarily be a strategic decision. But the implementation can take many forms. Here are a few of them found in companies that want to be among the first to read those 'weak signals' from the marketplace, spot an important new trend, a new competitor, or a family of new technologies:

- An annual selection of conferences, trade fairs, professional shows, national and international symposiums in which it will participate, nomination of those who will attend, and setting of objectives for the participants (papers to deliver, summary of proceedings to write, internal conferences on what was learned at such events).

- Annual selection of professional associations or other organized groups the company wishes to belong to, the designation of the persons to participate, and the role they should play. An important follow-on to these outside forays is again the distribution inside the company of the information and insights collected.

- The identification of the leading companies and the leading countries for its industry, and measures to ensure that employees at various levels are aware of progress there.

- Setting of clear objectives for gathering intelligence or information for all those who are concerned – the sales force on a continuing basis, the technical or managerial staffs each time they venture to an outside event.

- The creation of strategic monitoring teams to follow

specific forces in the marketplace (Japanese competition, for example), or teams to stay abreast of specific technologies such as biotechnology or new materials.

- Participation in venture capital funds to keep in touch with leading-edge technologies.

These are some of the most useful means for building a business intelligence system. Of course the true worth of the system will depend on the care taken in the earliest stages to determine what main themes to monitor. Secondly, it is crucial that the information be shared internally in the most effective way. Who needs to know, and why? The mere fact that a business intelligence system must be thoroughly planned helps transform the company, and moves it closer to becoming a Type 3 company.

9   Management by wandering around

MBWA, popularized by Hewlett-Packard, is obviously only one part of H-P's system for staying in touch with what is going on in the company. Each manager, each employee who has others reporting to him, is required to leave his office at least once a day and talk informally with three or four direct subordinates. The object is to ensure real contact, for there can be no real dialogue without this kind of openness. Of course MBWA is not enough by itself. The whole area of two-way communication must be rethought, including the importance of informal relations. At Hewlett-Packard the MBWA system is supported by an open-door policy. No office is out of bounds. Anyone can walk into anyone's office without fear, without excessive deference. Lastly, there is a tradition that all employees address others by their first names only – from chairman to nightwatchman. This makes communication easier and thus more effective. It also creates an underlying system of equality among employees.

The dialogue can include many other measures, including a company newspaper that grants employees free access to its news columns, the location of coffee machines to bring together people from different departments, the placement of offices. These measures must not be dismissed as frivolous. Employees at the French company Cofremca, for example, have shown that the rational model, the controlled organization, does not work for them. In their professional relations they want more contact with people, they want to express their emotions. The quality of employees' contribution to the company will depend on the kind of organization within which they work. If the company is impersonal, dry, mechanistic, the employees will be punctual and obedient. If the company is open, communicative, fostering simple and straightforward relations, allowing employees to assert themselves in different ways, the employees are sure to demonstrate a higher degree of commitment and engagement.

This informality and taste for dialogue can be a strong component in a plan to evolve into a Type 3 company.

10 Developing co-operation with small and medium-sized companies

Lesieur has been successful in this important area of building co-operation, so we shall focus on that experience as a model for others to consider. A few years ago Lesieur embarked on a project to create such a network, and called it by an unusual name – 'bountiful expansion' (*le foisonnement* in French). The word itself is more allusive than precise. It evokes a sense of abundance or expansion.

The name fits. It is a form of flexible growth that combines development, employment and innovation that are still compatible with ordinary methods of achieving industrial growth.

Frequently large companies approach small and medium-sized ones only to devour, absorb or strangle them. Sometimes the attack suits the smaller firm. The struggle for survival is over, monthly payroll or other deadlines are no longer a worry, the 'difficult adventure' is a thing of the past. Energies can be devoted to the smoother joys of the organization and to its control systems – in a word, to management.

But in the process of absorption, by whatever means, two

values indispensable to the competitive company – employment and innovation – are diminished, the former because
takeovers inevitably lead to cutbacks as duplication is
eliminated, and the latter because after the takeover all
innovation becomes part of the parent's strategy, so that
the smaller company settles down comfortably in the tran-
quillizing peace of management control. Employees, without
realizing it, begin to unlearn the innovative reflexes that had
been so important to survival when they were fighting for
markets alone. The loss of innovative power is a tragedy,
because it is precisely within these smaller firms that ideas
for the new products of tomorrow are born and nurtured.

The Lesieur group has had the good sense to see these
dangers of 'imperialistic diversification' and to opt for
'associative diversification' instead. Lesieur has sought out
the most dynamic and innovative companies in its three main
activities – edible oils, prepared foods and household cleaning
products – and helped them 'change gears'. The smaller companies will make up a large network around Lesieur and
by the early or mid-1990s all will share the following
advantages:

- Innovations from the small companies will benefit
  Lesieur, for example by channelling their new products
  into Lesieur's national distribution network.

- The smaller companies will create new jobs, as collaboration with Lesieur increases sales.

The concept seems simple enough, but it must develop with
a delicate balance. First of all, the large company setting
up the network must have a clear strategy in mind, for diversification is not an end in itself. Once the target areas for
diversification are chosen, the smaller associate companies
must be identified. And they must meet certain criteria: technical innovation must be among their assets, or in development; they must be sound financially and in personnel terms;
the management team must be young enough to carry through
a development programme (and not in need of a partner
to solve a succession problem for an ageing generation of

managers); and the team must have growth ambitions. These criteria will limit the field of selection considerably.

Yet Lesieur is building its network of associates little by little, holding its partners to a series of established rules. New members are told that the association is part of a development strategy, not a charity, and that in order to work it should be beneficial to both parties. Lesieur brings several advantages to the association: technical assistance through its laboratories, R & D facilities, production capacity, marketing expertise, distribution network, export knowhow, financing, and managerial skills. In return Lesieur expects the smaller associates to do their part in providing an expansion of its product line, new brand names, access to the new technologies developed privately, penetration of new local markets, and new managerial talent.

In the first two years Lesieur made associates of three smaller firms totalling about 500 employees. This is only a beginning. It will expand and produce synergistic benefits in the strategic areas chosen. Of course this programme will succeed only if all partners are guaranteed fairness and freedom of manoeuvre, and if their innovations are truly put into practice.

It is the genuine mutual advantage of the partners that makes this strategy so attractive. The more traditional measures being implemented today – conversion to new sectors, cutbacks in personnel, efforts to stimulate one activity while withdrawing from others – these are defensive strategies that, at best, only soften the effect of contraction. But the offensive strategy of companies like Lesieur has a better chance to develop innovation, competitiveness *and* employment – all of which European industry needs at this juncture.

Conclusion

Shared mission, four-speed approach, reactivity, total quality, phantom enterprise, the five zeros, interlinkage and 'bountiful expansion' – enough new terminology to make some readers smile. But there is good reason to create new labels: the concepts are new.

The task of management today is far removed from that of Taylor's day or those of his successors in the 1960s and 1970s. We are concerned with the Type 3 company, equipped to prosper in the new business environment. What is new about it? Every company today functions in an economic environment that is becoming more and more international. Industrial processes and procedures are more and more complex and interconnected. New technologies appear on the scene with greater frequency, and new competitive pressures arise from countries previously insignificant industrially, breaking down the old equilibrium and the old captive markets. This process in turn upsets employment levels throughout the industrialized world. The future belongs to those who understand new technologies and the value of informality, to those who anticipate, react swiftly, guarantee high quality, and do not attempt to win entirely alone. The future belongs to those who do not drag their feet, to those who mobilize the intelligence and enthusiasm of all employees, to those who build alliances.

It is perhaps not surprising that this Type 3 company has emerged on opposite shores of the Pacific Ocean. California, like Japan, is close to the spectacle of the great new industrial capacity of the South-east Asian economies. These smaller countries, with their immense talent for imitation, act as a kind of driving force behind the real leaders – California and Japan. The leaders are 'condemned' to perpetual acceleration, a diet of permanent innovation, and the constant search for alliances. The only means of staying ahead in the race is to harness the intelligence of men and women who are constantly better educated, better informed, and give them more responsibility, more say in the company's decisions; and, in addition, form a network rich and dense in relations with other companies that offer complementary strengths. These alliances create economies of scale, compensatory profits to offset losses, and act as a cushion against shocks in the marketplace; they also allow firms to lead joint offensives, and to develop managers who are better armed for the more complex environment in which they will have to live.

Does the Type 3 approach produce frenetic managerial types? Not at all. The kind of people who innovate, improve quality and take wise decisions are men and women capable of relaxing, of being open-minded and of stepping back from the daily pressures of business to look at a problem from a distance. Type 3 companies are responsive to the views of others, to the socio-cultural values unique to each group.

On opposite sides of the Pacific Ocean people have rediscovered how essential is the contribution of each individual, how the human resource is at the heart of economic performance. It may be that these insights are rooted in pragmatism and a yearning for efficiency, but that does not lessen their importance. These human resources will be decisive in the competitive struggle. The Type 3 companies put people at the centre of their networks of technology and information.

This fundamental change has already taken place in some companies in the West. Let us hope that the urgency of the need today will help us rediscover what the American model of the 1950s and a growing bureaucracy have made us forget: the human side of industry and the strength of our very considerable talents. With those two forces at work Type 3 companies should be able to achieve levels of performance never seen before.

APPENDICES

Appendix A Quality circles at Nippon Steel

The material in this appendix is taken from a booklet distributed by Nippon Steel Corp. (NSC) in 1983. We offer it as a document that sheds light on Nippon Steel's strategy for motivation and participation of employees in the wide variety of initiatives for progress. The document illustrates the ability of the Japanese to move from concepts of product quality or worklife quality to concrete applications that actually result in progress. It also illustrates Japanese perseverance as a key to success, and their great capacity for mobilizing employees to solve problems. After ten years of development NSC had organized quality circles (Figure A.1) for 46 521 out of the total payroll of 69 926. About 26 000 problems are solved each year by these employee groups.

Advantages of QCs

Quality circles are a permanent activity in which small groups of volunteers of the same level consider problems of their choice and seek creative solutions.

Each QC participant improves his ability to solve problems of increasing importance by using his creative capacities. He respects his fellow-worker, and seeks to improve the quality

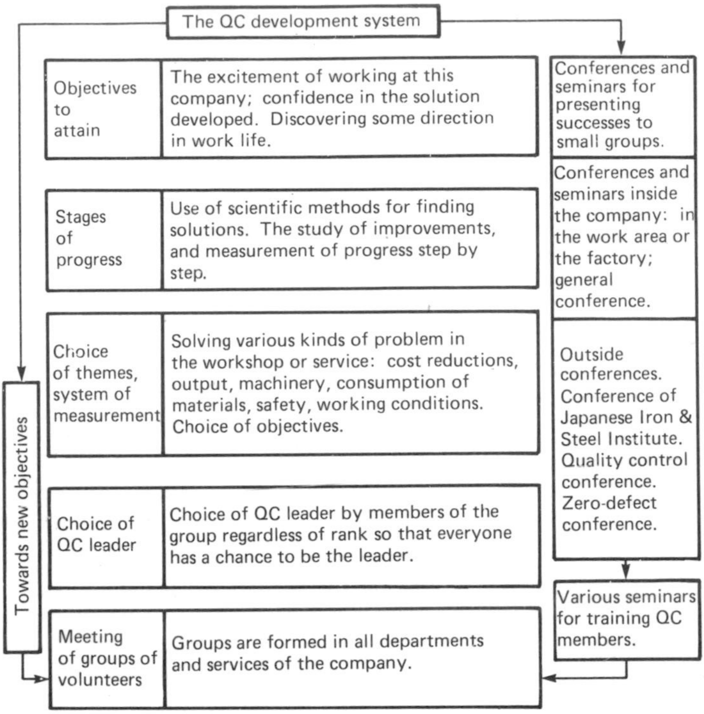

Figure A.1   Diagram of system for developing quality circles

of life in the work area. All QCs contribute to the development of the enterprise and of the entire company.

Strategy for effectiveness

Employees must be given maximum latitude to use their potential and to concentrate on solving the problems rather than meeting fixed economic objectives.

Action steps

1   Give each person concrete tasks; raise qualifications of QC participants; create group projects.

2   Raise the qualifications of the managers; improve the effectiveness of participation by functional specialists.

3   Foster the transfer of technical knowledge and the penetration of technical progress.

4   Reduce all costs, particularly energy costs.

5   Develop solidarity within the company.

The main orientations of progress

1   Management is based on the respect of others.

2   The most advanced training to be made available throughout the company.

3   Lifetime employment.

4   Salaries keyed to seniority.

5   In-house trade unions.

6   Training of newly hired personnel to prepare them for the growth strategies of NSC, making them especially aware of the following points:

- quality control,
- industrial engineering,
- 'protective' maintenance,
- automation,
- increasing the power and output of equipment,
- computers.

7   Information and training throughout employees' careers, by these means:

- career path covering several functions and companies of the group,
- exchange of information on new techniques, especially in internal conferences,

- improvement of the effectiveness of management systems,

- development of relations with the outside environment,

- seminars on individual behaviour,

- improvement of the quality of life inside the enterprise,

- study of problems caused by the recession and of the real battles that must be won,

- search for solutions to problems posed scientifically.

How to help the orientations for progress take hold

1   Ensure that the new directions are fully understood by all – from top management down the ladder to the lowest job.

2   Define the criteria for the promotion of all managers; organize conferences to show the increments of progress achieved by any employee.

3   Put in place training programmes at all levels, especially at the level of the bosses.

4   Define for each work area specific progress objectives, always ensuring coherence with the company's strategy for progress.

5   Develop these activities while respecting the principle of the volunteer, of free thought and free speech.

6   Bring to the QC activity all the required training, technical assistance, advice and other means.

7   Raise the morale of employees by allowing them to participate freely in meetings, conferences and training sessions, internal and external.

Data and results

Tables A.1 and A.2 and Figure A.2 present the effect of Nippon Steel's use of quality circles.

Table A.1
Conferences on quality

Nature	Frequency	Objectives
General, company-wide	Once a year	Presentation of progress and exchange of views and experiences among groups of workers and management. These conferences help show the way for progress in the company.
Department level	Annually in each department	Presentations focusing on techniques and the improvement of equipment. This helps in the exchange of technology and ultimately improves the quality of products.
Workshop level	Twice a year in the work area	Mainly encounters of technicians to exchange experiences, recognition of their determinant role as those who make the quality circles work.

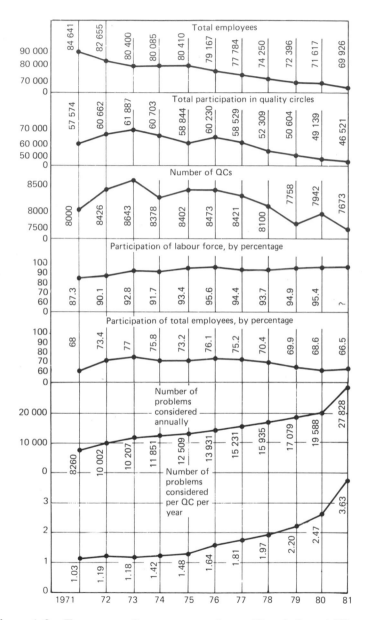

Figure A.2   Ten years of perseverance in quality circles at Nippon Steel, and their results

Table A.2
Results of quality circles, Nippon Steel, 1982

Number of problems solved by QCs
Total: 27 828

Breakdown by type of problem (%)

Productivity	30.9
Safety	22.0
Product quality	11.9
Environmental conditions	4.1
Miscellaneous	4.4
Cost reductions	26.7
	100.00

Breakdown of cost reductions, by type (%)

Energy conservation	8.6
Output	3.4
Raw materials	3.3
Intermediate materials	0.7
Saving in work time	0.9
Miscellaneous	9.8

Appendix B Group management services at Nippon Steel

NSC has created at its headquarters level an office of assistance for its affiliated companies to provide them with management services. The unit produced a pamphlet to promote its services. Some excerpts are given below.

Object of management services

Management of the enterprise must be constantly renewed

The big problems that all companies face today are 'How to win the competitive battles' and 'How to cope with the evolution in management in a period of slow growth and rapid technical innovation'.

Where there is an enterprise, there is a problem. Things are going normally, sales are not bad. But close examination will reveal many problems. They emerge in various ways:

- They do not appear on the surface, but they exist.

- They are not big problems when considered individually, but they become important when viewed from the perspective of the company as a whole.

This phenomenon is due to the following factors:

- Waste problems exist, even if they are not noticeable.

- Waste develops invisibly in terms of cost and time.

- At least as a precaution, it is important to view the company scientifically and with fresh eyes, even when problems are not directly apparent. This is of course even more true in companies where problems are emerging.

Management services can be used in the following cases

- When productivity is declining and sales are not increasing.

- When product quality is unstable and the rate of output of the production process is good.

- When raw materials and products are not 'flowing' well; the output of machines and equipment is poor.

- When there is a delay in delivery of products from time to time.

- When there is a desire to conserve energy but not the expertise to accomplish it.

- When a reduction in costs is desired, or accomplished, but results are below expectations.

- When some self-management schemes are needed, or have been introduced, but are not working well.

- When the climate at the factory is rather gloomy, or employees are not very dynamic.

- When workers need to be taught the techniques of industrial engineering in order to act effectively in programmes for better productivity and reduction of costs.

- When an installation is to be renovated or enlarged, and surplus equipment is to be utilized or other equipment sold off.

In all these cases, do not hesitate to contact 'Management Services':

- Our specialized staff will study your needs, identify the problems, and help you plan for improvements.

- We can help you launch training programmes in industrial engineering, QCs, zero-defect programmes or others (such as self-management).

- To ensure optimum use of idle equipment and machines in the company or its affiliates, we can provide information to you and serve as intermediary. We have our knowhow and the benefit of our experience.

Inside the company, in our steel plants, we have for many years introduced and managed factory analysis, training cycles, apprenticeships and group activities. We have built up an enormous wealth of knowledge and considerable results.

In addition, since June 1977 (date of creation of the Office of Assistance to Affiliates) we have:

- Performed plant analysis in sixty-three companies.

- Provided advice for the introduction of self-management (decentralization) schemes in sixty-two companies.

- Training in industrial engineering techniques; thirty-seven groups, totalling 1252 persons.

Appendix C   What is productivity?

The Japanese Productivity Centre was founded in 1955 as a tripartite organization, a private, non-profit group representing management, labour and academia, dedicated to promoting productivity in Japanese industry. It was rather like the Mecca of productivity, and it was expected to produce the most original and sophisticated – the best – solutions to the problem. Yet the Centre's declarations on the theme of productivity are surprisingly simple.

Three basic principles

1   In the long term, productivity improvements should increase employment. During a transition period, however, before the effects are felt, the government and the population, in order to minimize frictions that might interfere with the functioning of the national economy, should co-operate to take appropriate measures, such as the transfer of excess workers in some regions to other regions that are short of labour, to avoid unemployment.

2   In the development of concrete measures to increase productivity, labour and management, in conformity with the conditions in force in their respective com-

panies, should co-operate in discussions, studies and collaboration on such measures.

3 The results of increased productivity, after having fulfilled the requirements of the national economy, must be distributed equally to the managers, workers and consumers.

Above all, productivity is a state of mind

It is an attitude of progress and constant improvement. It is the certainty that one can do better tomorrow than yesterday.

It is the willingness to improve the present situation so that it *seems* good and *really is* good. It is the constant adaptation of social and economic life to changing conditions; it is the continuous effort to apply new technologies and new methods; it is faith in human progress.

Index

Numerals in *italics* refer to figures

119